KIM BRIGHT

Dumb B.I.T.C.H.

The Smart Woman's Guide to Decode Emotional Terrorism
& Narcissistic Abuse

Kim Brightness

This book was professionally typeset on Reedsy.
Find out more at reedsy.com

To those I spoke of before I knew you existed.

Contents

Preface

Meanwhile, every survivor remembers the exact moment she woke up to the truth.

"Dumb bitch!"

The words felt like two hand grenades exploding simultaneously in my face. For a few seconds, I sat at my desk in shock. I'd never been called a *dumb bitch* before in my life. It was one of those *"where were you when _____ happened?"* moments you never forget.

By the time my ears stopped ringing, and the back-and-forth yelling quieted down, there was no way I was going to let him pimp-walk out of my office after cursing me out. So, I came up with the hardest clap-back in modern clap-back history:

> *"And if you call me a dumb bitch again, I'm gonna write a book called 'Dumb Bitch' and help other women in these toxic relationships!"*

Immediately, my inner critic fired off.

"Girl!

Really?

***That** was the best clap back you had?*

I'ma write a book...?

Were you trying to prove him right?

*How **dumb** was that?!?"*

I spent the next hours, days, weeks being all super creative with words I *could've* said in the moment that was now gone.

Gone.

That's the concept I had the most trouble with during my toxic, twenty-eight-year marriage—especially without a book like this to help make sense of what was going on.

How do I get "gone" from a narcissistic relationship I love that's hell-bent on sucking the life out of me? How do I get "gone" from the trauma that molded me to gladly settle for crumbs for over thirty years together, while my emotional, mental, and psychological health lay lifeless in a chalk outline?

Gone.

Why did it take more than a decade from that faithful day in my office to realize that my identity and self-esteem were "gone", and I was on auto-pilot in covenant by myself?

How do I thrive in this new reality that the relationship is "gone", knowing I only sacrificed, people-pleased, and forgave my way back to singlehood?

Where do you buy storage bins big enough to pack all your memories, hopes, and dreams for a future that's "gone" and a present with only me here?

Here.

That's where the answers lie. After everything I've been through—domestic violence, infidelity + social media humiliation, false accusations, a 15-month trial in Superior Court accused by the ex of contempt, slander, and abusing his mother, even a judge's directive that halted *written communications* of this book—I'm still here!

That day in my office, I made a vow. If he was going to call me a "dumb bitch", I would re-purpose those words into a positive weapon for women trapped in their darkest moments of emotional terrorism and narcissistic abuse. I would break down the tactics, expose the lies, illuminate truth, and show other women how to get free.

Yes, those two words, those two hand grenades exploded again; the book you're now holding is that vow in print. A promise kept.

I didn't write this book from the sidelines. I wrote it from the battlefield. I know what it feels like to question your sanity, to stay silent out of fear, to beg for scraps of love that keep your soul famished. I know how it feels to be in love with a person who slowly erases you while smiling to the world—and the world unwittingly smiles back.

And, I also know what it takes to thrive. To decode the manipulation. To see the narcissistic traits for what they are. To stop defending, justifying, enabling, and apologizing for someone who feeds on your low self-esteem. I know what it takes to stop settling and kill the pride in my strong, caterpillar muscles to soar with the strength of a butterfly.

I wrote this book not because of a degree or a title. But because I survived. I studied the tactics. I put language to the pain. And as a coach, I've helped other women escape the same hell.

So, if you've ever been called out of your name... if you've ever felt like you couldn't trust your own reality... if you've ever walked on eggshells until your feet bled... if you've ever asked yourself, *"I wonder which person will show up today?"*—this book is for you.

You are not crazy. You are not weak. And, you are not a dumb bitch.

You are stronger than you know.

And by the time you read the truth in these pages, the truth will set you free, too.

Working Definitions

Emotional Terrorism (n.)

ih-**moh**-sh*uh*-nl **ter**-*uh*-riz-*uh*m

1 : any intimidation or manipulation that *threatens* to produce or *produces* what your heart fears most in the relationship.

Narcissistic Abuse (n.)

*nahr-suh-**sis**-tik uh-**byoos***

2 : psychological abuse marked by gaslighting, control, lack of empathy, and exploitation that erodes identity.

B.I.T.C.H.

Beautiful
Intelligent
Tenacious
Courageous
High-Value
woman

Introduction

"My people are destroyed for lack of knowledge." - Hosea 4:6

Sis, if you've picked up this book, chances are you're exhausted.

You're tired of walking on eggshells, tired of second-guessing yourself, tired of feeling like you're losing your mind in a relationship that should bring you peace. You're tired of conventional relationship advice that doesn't work with someone who isn't playing by *normal* relationship rules.

You're not crazy. You're not too sensitive. You're not asking for too much.

You're in the game of Cat and mouse, and it's time to learn the rules so you can escape the madness.

The Cat and Mouse Metaphor

Throughout this book, I refer to the emotional abuser or narcissistic partner as "the Cat" and the victim as "the mouse." This isn't to diminish your strength or suggest you're weak. It's to illustrate the predatory dynamic that exists in narcissistic abuse relationships—one person hunting while the other survives, one person playing while the other suffers, one person in control while the other scrambles to keep up.

The Cat enjoys the chase. They thrive on the power, the control, the emotions they can manipulate. They're not trying to catch the Mouse to love it; they're trying to catch it to possess it, control it, and ultimately devour it.

The Mouse, meanwhile, is focused on survival. Every decision is made to avoid the Cat's claws, prevent the Cat's anger, or earn the Cat's approval. The Mouse doesn't realize (yet) that no amount of "purrfect" behavior will satisfy the Cat, whose primary goal is the hunt itself.

How This Book Is Structured

This book follows a deliberate journey from recognition to freedom, organized into five distinct sections:

Section I: Recognizing the Game (Chapters 1-5)
Here, you'll learn to identify the Cat and mouse dynamic, understand the rules of emotional terrorism, recognize the signs you're in an emotionally abusive relationship, and understand how people-pleasing becomes a survival mechanism that ultimately makes you a target.

Section II: Understanding the Cat (Chapters 6-9)
This section explores the psychology behind emotional abuse. You'll learn about narcissistic behavior patterns, the cycle of abuse, how abusers recruit others to assist them, and the spiritual dimension behind emotional terrorism.

Section III: Healing the Wounded Mouse (Chapters 10-13)
Before you can reclaim your power, you must heal your wounds. This section addresses how to break trauma bonds, practice biblical forgiveness, reconnect with your authentic identity, and experience the awakening that leads to change.

Section IV: Reclaiming the Mouse's Power (Chapters 14-16)
Now you're ready to take back control. You'll learn to build an escape plan, understand the recovery timeline, and establish boundaries that protect your newfound freedom.

Section V: Game Over - This Is Your New Life (Chapters 17-20)
The final section is about thriving beyond survival. You'll learn to declare "game over" to the toxic dynamic, reclaim joy as an act of resistance, create healthy romantic relationships, and embrace the abundant life you were always meant to live.

Understanding the Special Sections

Throughout each chapter, you'll encounter two recurring sections designed to deepen your understanding and reinforce your progress:

Cat Tactics Decoded
These sections expose specific manipulation strategies used by emotional abusers. Think of them as a decoder ring for toxic behavior. When you understand the tactic, you can't be fooled by it. These sections will help you recognize manipulation in real-time and understand that the confusing, hurtful behavior you've experienced follows predictable patterns. You're not dealing with someone who's just having a bad day or going through a rough patch - you're dealing with someone who uses calculated strategies to maintain control.

Mouse Traps
These sections identify common pitfalls that keep victims stuck in abusive dynamics. Even with the best intentions, it's easy to fall into patterns or make choices that enable the abuse to continue. Mouse Traps help you recognize when you're about to step into quicksand disguised as solid ground. They're not about blaming you for the abuse - that responsibility lies solely with the abuser. They're about empowering you so you can make choices that serve your healing and freedom.

The Biblical Foundation

This book approaches healing through a biblical lens. As a disciple of Jesus Christ, I would love for you to have a personal relationship with Him (see Appendix prayer), but you don't have to share my faith to benefit from these principles. The wisdom found in Scripture about human nature, healthy relationships, forgiveness, and personal worth speaks to universal truths about how we're created to live and love.

I believe that God's heart breaks when women are mistreated, manipulated, and made to feel worthless. The abundant life Jesus promised isn't just about eternity - it's about living with dignity, purpose, and joy right here, right now. You were created for love that builds you up, not tears you down. You were "fearfully and wonderfully made" for relationships that honor your worth, not exploit your kindness.

If biblical references aren't part of your belief system, simply focus on the practical wisdom and psychological insights. The strategies for healing and empowerment are sound, regardless of your spiritual background.

A Word About Triggers and Self-Care

This book addresses difficult topics, including emotional abuse, manipulation, trauma, domestic violence, and the psychological impact of toxic relationships. Some content may be triggering if you're still in an abusive situation or early in your healing journey.

Please prioritize your emotional safety as you read. Take breaks when you need them. Skip sections that feel too overwhelming right now - you can always return to them when you're ready. Consider reading with the support of a therapist, counselor, or trusted friend who understands your situation.

If you're currently in physical danger, please contact the National Domestic Violence Hotline at 1-800-799-7233 or visit thehotline.org. Your safety is the top priority.

Meeting You Where You Are

Wherever you are in your journey, this book meets you there:

If you're still in the relationship and questioning your reality: The early chapters will help you identify what you're experiencing and validate your concerns. You're not imagining things, and you're not overreacting.

If you've recently left or are planning to leave: The middle sections will help you understand the dynamics you've experienced and begin the healing process. You'll find practical guidance for safely moving forward.

If you've been out of the relationship for a while but still struggling: The later chapters focus on deep healing, reclaiming your identity, and building a thriving life. Healing isn't linear, and it's never too late to address unresolved trauma.

If you're helping someone else in this situation: This book will give you insight into what your loved one is experiencing and how you can best support them. Sometimes understanding the dynamics is the first step toward offering meaningful help.

How to Get the Most from This Book

Read at your own pace. This isn't a race. Some chapters may require multiple readings or the time to process. Honor your emotional capacity and don't rush the journey.

Keep a journal. Consider writing down insights, reactions, and reflections as you read. The act of writing can help you process emotions and track your growth.

Apply the concepts gradually. This book is a "guide" filled with conceptual lists and frameworks. Don't try to implement everything at once. Choose one or two strategies that resonate with you and practice them until they become natural.

Seek support. Sometimes healing happens best in community. Consider joining a support group, working with a therapist, or connecting with other survivors who understand your experience.

Trust your instincts. If something in this book doesn't feel right for your situation, trust that feeling. You know your circumstances better than anyone else.

Celebrate your Courage. The fact that you're reading this book means you're already taking steps toward freedom. I applaud you. That takes tremendous Courage, and you should be proud of yourself.

Your Journey Starts Here

The cat-and-mouse game has rules, but so does freedom. You're about to learn both.

This book isn't just about surviving emotional terrorism and narcissistic abuse - it's about transforming from victim to survivor to thriver. It's about remembering who you were before someone convinced you that you were less than who you are. It's about reclaiming your voice, your power, and your right to be treated with dignity and respect.

The woman you're becoming - stronger, wiser, more discerning - is already within you. Let's wake her up. She's been there all along, waiting for you to remember her worth and step into her power.

Your healing matters. Your freedom matters. Your future matters.

So, let's begin.

I

SECTION I: RECOGNIZING THE GAME

1

Chapter 1: The Cat and Mouse Phenomenon

"He sent his word and healed them; he rescued them from their traps." - *Psalm 107:20 CSB*

Sis, have you ever watched a cat stalk its prey? The calculated patience. The elongated torso and blink-less focus. The deceptive quietness in every paw print, all culminating in explosive action. There's something almost hypnotic about the way a cat hunts. Could this explain why the mesmerized mouse always gets trapped?

Imagine waking up one random morning to discover you've been cast in a role you never auditioned for: the Mouse in an elaborate game of "cat-and-mouse". Only this isn't happening in some random barnyard or back alley. The stage is set in your own bedroom, kitchen, and living room. It's happening in real-time via text messages and voice notes, in whispered conversations at 4 A.M. and knock-out-drag-out fights by noon. This alternative reality happens in the numb space between "I love you" and "You don't even look good enough to be my wife!"

Welcome to the high-stakes game of emotional terrorism, where two days actually *are* alike in the most stressful and manipulative ways.

Now, you may be thinking, "Terrorism, Kim? Really? Isn't that a bit dramatic?"

Let me ask you this: Have you ever walked on eggshells in your own home? Have you ever rehearsed conversations in your head, strategizing every word, trying to anticipate all the potential landmines? Have you ever felt your stomach drop when you heard the garage door open, signaling his return after he left upset about something you didn't do? Have you ever seen his name appear on the caller ID, and now all of a sudden, you're afraid to answer the phone? Have you ever had to lock yourself in the bathroom, go to sleep with headphones, or leave the house altogether to get away from a verbal firestorm? Have you ever been so confused by someone's behavior that you questioned your own sanity, your own reality?

If you answered yes to any of these questions, Ma'am, you're not being dramatic. You're being terrorized.

The relationship is characterized by toxic cycles of the Cat's terror and near captures, and the Mouse's counter-attacks and repeated escapes. It's worth noting that there are moments when the Mouse doesn't even need an elaborate escape plan; the Cat playfully and willfully *releases* the mouse after capture, only to commence the chase again. The mouse is often confused by how swiftly a peaceful olive branch can turn into a cruel weapon of mass destruction. Emotions can shift from jubilation to confusion, relief to dread in a matter of moments. And, if the Mouse has a propensity for people-pleasing, she often experiences a wave of self-imposed anxieties, trying to appease someone who is simultaneously hell-bent on destroying her spirit.

The term "emotional terrorism" isn't meant to sensationalize or exaggerate toxic relationships. It's meant to accurately name the emotional, psychological, and spiritual warfare experienced when one person systematically breaks down another's sense of self, reality, and safety.

Think about what you fear most in your relationship. Maybe it's a fear of abandonment, fear of infidelity, or simply the fear of losing them and being alone. An emotional terrorist, or strongly narcissistic person, seeks to destroy your spirit by using intimidation and manipulation that threatens to produce what you fear most (read that again).

It doesn't matter if they have the means, ability, or intention to carry out the threat or not. They will activate sleeper cells in your psyche—"If you don't want to {*insert demand*}, then somebody else will!", or "Keep on {*insert your attempt at a boundary or standing up for yourself*} and you're going to find yourself alone!"

This brand of terror not only applies to what you fear most for yourself, but also what you fear most for them. For example, if the Cat has a predisposition to suicide ideation, trust me, no one will threaten to un-alive themselves faster than a Cat caught cheating. The warfare inflicted on your emotions, i.e., your heart balancing the torment of infidelity and the threat of their death, would be terrifying. The mission is to disturb your mental and emotional well-being and chip away at your self-worth, all while producing seeds of panic that grow into deeper emotional instability.

Just as domestic or international terrorism uses violence to control through fear, emotional terrorism uses psychological manipulation to achieve the same end. At the heart of the cat-and-mouse game lies this declaration of jihad—a non-negotiable duty to inflict emotional violence—that terrorizes the heart, mind, body, and soul of the Mouse.

Decoding the Rules of the Game

Every game has rules, even toxic ones. The rules may be unwritten, or unspoken, but they will be enforced without warning or grace periods.

When the stage is set for the game of cat-and-mouse, the mouse doesn't get to write, contribute to, or approve the rules—the Cat does. However, you most definitely need to be able to decode the rules of engagement. According to Section 1.0 of the Cat's Playbook, *the rules imposed on the Mouse do not apply to the Cat, and the rights and privileges given to the Cat do not apply to the Mouse.* If you go into this game thinking that the Cat will play fair, that there will be balance and empathy for your feelings, you will find yourself crushed under the weight of perceived love mixed with actual hate. And that, Ma'am, is a combination that will make your head spin so fast, your grip on reality will slip from your blistered fingertips.

Understanding these rules, should you choose to accept the part, is the first step toward recognizing you're playing a game designed with your destruction in mind. Let's take a brief look.

Rule #1: The Cat always initiates.

How did you get here? Where did your invitation come from?

The game begins when the Cat selects you. Not haphazardly or by a random choice. Cats are particular about their prey.

They want a challenge, but not an impossible one. They want a Mouse with enough spirit to make the chase interesting, but not so much spirit that they might actually lose. They want Intelligence, but the kind they can outsmart, not the kind that outshines them. They want enough Beauty that can be paraded around to impress others, but the kind they can also convince is ugly without them when the time is right. They want strength, the kind with broad, soft shoulders that can carry them and their goals, but also the kind they can gradually weaken with a toxic mixture of love bombs and slurs.

So, you've been watched. Studied. The Cat has cased you like a jewelry store slated for a pending heist. Your worth, far above rubies and diamonds, is under surveillance. Where has unhealed trauma left her most vulnerable? Through which door did her daddy abandon her? She has guards around her most precious gems, but how can they be distracted, or better yet, paid off with adoration, praise, or mind-blowing sex? The emotional terrorist has collected all the data needed to conclude—you are the one. Time to roll out the red ~~flags~~ carpet and welcome you to the game.

The stage is set, and your personal invitation warms your heart. It's often sealed in an answer to your unspoken prayer for help, guidance, connection, or support in a certain area of your life. Well, whaddya know—the Cat is an expert and has access to resources for the missing piece of the puzzle. Void filled.

In short, they want you. The Beautiful, Intelligent, Tenacious, Courageous, High-value woman. The B.I.T.C.H. The one with endearing traits sprinkled with a dash of unhealed trauma, family issues, and hidden insecurities that the Cat can smell on your soul.

Rule #2: The game has distinct phases (H-P-R)

First comes the "**hunt**"—what many in the mental health community call "love bombing." This is when the Cat showers you with attention, affection, gifts, and admiration to form a deep, emotional bond with you, quickly. You're perfect. You're everything he's ever wanted. You're not like other women. You understand him in a way no one else does. All of this adoration waters your soul in spaces that may be dry or brittle, or it fertilizes a seed of pride buried deep in your heart. Either way, you're hooked on the high because it feels so good to finally be appreciated, seen, and adored.

Then comes the "**pounce**"—entrapment by the first betrayal, the first cruel comment. The first time they call you out of your name or humiliate you in public. It's shocking. It comes out of nowhere, often unprovoked. You don't know who this guy is, and this intrusion by *Mr. Hyde* is as disorienting as whiplash from a rear-end collision you never saw coming. Never in a million years would you have ever expected the Cat to treat you in this manner, and you would be hard-pressed to convince anyone else that he did what he did.

But before you can fully process what happened, or hold them accountable for their actions, here comes phase three—they "**release**" you. You're presented with the perfect motion picture apology that crosses all the t's and dots all the i's you were going to bring to their attention. How impressive is their contrition and self-awareness! They bring flowers. They snot cry. They promise it will never happen again. Relieved to have your loving partner back again, you believe them.

And the *hunt* begins again. Your pleasure chemical (dopamine) levels shoot through the roof. Then the *pounce*, again. Then the *release*, again. Then the...

Rule #3: The Cat controls the clock.

One of the most disorienting aspects of this game is its unpredictability. The Cat decides *when* the hunt begins, *when* the pounce happens, and *when* the temporary release is granted. And of course, every *when* is dictated by a universal *if*—*if* the Cat decides to hunt, pounce, or release based on their rules of engagement. You're constantly reacting, never able to act on a solid footing. Your life becomes dictated by their fluctuating moods, their needs, and their schedule.

Here's what a typical week in the game might look like. Monday might be perfect—dinner together, genuine conversation, physical intimacy, great sex. Tuesday might be the silent treatment for a reason you know nothing about. Wednesday, when he finally does speak to you, might bring accusations that you're cheating or you don't love him, followed by tearful apologies and sexual advances by sundown. Thursday might be so normal you start to think you imagined the chaos from the previous days. By Friday, you're mentally and emotionally exhausted, confused, and desperately trying to figure out what you did to trigger this cycle.

But here's the truth: You didn't trigger anything. The game was designed this way from the start.

The Psychological Impact of the Game

Living in this perpetual state of uncertainty creates what psychologists call a *trauma bond* — a powerful, emotional attachment formed through repeated cycles of abuse and affection. The highs feel so high, they become addictive, especially after the turmoil of devastating lows. You just want to feel the love again. You just want to be free. The missing moments of peace and affection become worth *any* ransom price.

Your brain, desperate to make sense of all the chaos, begins to adapt. You develop hyper-vigilance, constantly scanning for signs of danger. Ultimately, the moments of peace you ransomed with kindness and people pleasing become the boogeyman you can't trust. The affection you craved betrays you. You become an unexpected expert at reading subtle shifts in tone, facial expressions, and body language. You learn to anticipate needs before they're expressed. Crumbs of kindness satisfy your soul like a feast. You become smaller, quieter, more accommodating, more pleasing.

In psychological terms, the game exposes you to the cause and effects of *intermittent reinforcement*. This strategic and powerful form of behavioral conditioning happens when rewards (in this case, love and affection) are given unpredictably, causing the person to try even harder to earn them.

It's the same principle that keeps gamblers "bonded" like glue to slot machines. With every pull, there's anticipation, a rush of excitement that *this* could be the moment. This next pull could be the big payout of your dreams. Without surprise, you adopt the mindset that, "If I don't play, I won't win." Now, sometimes you win, and the Cat surprises you with an easy payout of love and affection. Sometimes you lose, and the Cat pounces on you even harder than before. But the possibility of reward, mixed with toxic optimism and displaced faith, keeps you playing long after you should have exited the game.

Invisible Wounds and Unlimited Lives

"But he's never hit me," many women trapped in the game of cat-and-mouse say. "He's never physically hurt me."

Physical abuse leaves visible evidence—bruises, broken bones, scars. Emotional abuse leaves invisible wounds that can be just as devastating, and often take longer to heal than visible ones. The wounds from emotional terrorism may be invisible to others, but they're painfully real to you, and can cause any of the following deeper issues:

- Depression and anxiety
- Post-traumatic stress disorder
- Chronic pain and other physical health problems
- Cognitive distortions and difficulty trusting your own perceptions
- Low self-worth and lack of true identity
- Difficulty forming healthy relationships in the future

Because the game demands that you develop such a toxic resistance to repeated emotional wounds, it diminishes your perception of reality—you're in serious danger, girl!

The longer you play, the more the cat-and-mouse game begins to feel like you're stuck in a wicked video game. The pounce doesn't hurt that bad after all, not for a player with unlimited *lives*. It doesn't matter what happens to *this* mouse, or how many times she fails the mission to please the Cat. The mouse will be given another "chance" to know and do better.

But what the game does not tell you is that every iteration of the mouse is weaker, more confused, and more damaged than the previous players. The mouse will never be as strong and confident as the day she was chosen for the game. And the Cat knows it.

Cat Tactics Decoded

Let's take a brief moment to look at some common tactics the Cat employs to maintain game control.

Gaslighting: *"That never happened. You're making things up again."*

Translation: I need you to doubt your reality so you'll accept mine.

Projection: *"You're so selfish. You never think about anyone but yourself."*

Translation: I'm describing myself but attributing these qualities to you to deflect attention from my behavior.

Isolation: *"Your friends don't really care about you. They're just using you."*

Translation: I need to separate you from your support system so you'll be completely dependent on me.

Moving the goalposts: *"Yes, I said that would make me happy, but what I really meant was…"*

Translation: I need to ensure you can never succeed or feel secure in meeting my expectations.

These tactics aren't random acts of meanness. They're calculated strategies from the emotional terrorist's playbook designed to maintain power and control.

Mouse Traps

As an Intelligent woman, you must be aware of common pitfalls that can keep you trapped in the game. Here are some early mouse traps intended to seal your fate:

Mistaking intensity for intimacy: The passionate beginning of these relationships often feels like deep connection. Is he really that into you after only one week? He's not. Real connection builds over time through consistent action, respect, and vulnerability.

Confusing jealousy with love: Being constantly monitored, questioned, or accused isn't a sign of passionate love. It's a sign of insecurity and control that won't be "cute" for long.

Believing you can fix them: Your love, patience, and understanding won't heal someone who doesn't recognize they're wounded, or doesn't want to change.

Comparing your situation to worse scenarios: "At least he doesn't hit me" or "At least we have financial stability" are thoughts that keep you accepting the unacceptable bare minimum.

Investing in potential rather than reality: You stay for who they could be, not who they consistently show themselves to be.

Breaking the Cycle

I won't pretend that the way out of this game is always quick, easy, or painless. Trauma bonds are real. The thoughts that terrorize you appear real. Your love—yes, even amid the chaos—is real.

But recognizing emotional terrorism for what it is represents a crucial first step that strips the game of some of its power. Understanding the rules helps you see that you've been set up to lose from the beginning—not because you're weak or stupid, but because there was a vulnerability that made you susceptible to the game.

In the chapters that follow, we'll explore how narcissistic relationships develop, why Intelligent women often stay in them longer than you might expect, and most importantly, how to repossess your power and ultimately tell the Cat: "Game over."

For now, I want you to hold onto one truth: This game does not dictate your worth, God does. It was always about the Cat's need for control. Your value as a Beautiful, Intelligent, Tenacious, Courageous, High-value woman (B.I.T.C.H.) remains intact, regardless of how long you've been playing the game.

The fact that you're reading these words means something within you recognizes the toxicity of your situation and is fighting to break free. That fighting spirit? That longing for more, for better? That's the real you, the you that existed before the game began, and the you that will emerge stronger when the game ends.

And it will end, when you're ready. I promise you that.

2

Chapter 2: When Love Becomes a Battlefield

"Look beneath the surface so you can judge correctly." - John 7:24 NLT

In a perfect world where romantic relationships are pure and simple, love is a sanctuary. In the real world—particularly in the world of narcissistic abuse or emotional terrorism—love is a battlefield, sis. And not the kind Pat Benatar sang about in the 80's. This is psychological and spiritual warfare with real casualties, real trauma, and real scars that linger long after the final shot is fired.

But here's the thing about this particular battlefield: you didn't know you were enlisting. There was no recruitment officer, no boot camp, no warning that you were about to enter a combat zone. Instead, there were roses. Candlelit dinners. Long walks and great conversation. Passionate declarations of love. Soul-mate talk. Future plans.

"How did I get here?" you might wonder, looking around at the smoking ruins of what was once a promising relationship. "When did our love turn into this?"

The answer is both simple and complex. It happened gradually, then suddenly.

Like the proverbial frog in slowly heating water, you didn't jump out of the pot immediately because the temperature rose so incrementally that by the time it was boiling, you'd lost your ability to recognize danger.

Let's trace that journey from romance to warfare, and understand how the Cat systematically transforms love into a weapon.

Green Flags vs. Red Flags: False Signage on the Battlefield

In healthy relationships—or what some call "green flag" relationships—certain behaviors signal safety, mutual respect, and genuine connection:

- You are seen and accepted the way God made you
- Your boundaries are acknowledged and honored
- You feel safe expressing your true thoughts and feelings
- Your partner celebrates your successes without jealousy
- Disagreements are handled with respect, not character assassination
- Responsibility and accountability are acknowledged without blame
- Loyalty and love don't change when *life happens*
- You maintain connections with friends and family
- You feel like yourself, only better, in their presence

In the Cat and mouse dynamic—let's call it "red flag" relationships—these healthy signals are initially mimicked with Oscar-worthy precision. As discussed in the last chapter, the Cat *studies* what makes the perfect partner and performs these behaviors flawlessly during the recruitment phase.

But mixed in with these counterfeit green flags are subtle red ones that, in retrospect, were warning you from the beginning to run:

- Love that feels too intense, too soon
- Excessive curiosity about your past relationships
- Subtle put-downs disguised as jokes or "honesty"
- Testing small boundaries to see if you'll enforce them
- Dramatic stories positioning them as either the victim or the hero
- Inconsistencies in their personal and employment histories

· An unusual interest in and empathy for your vulnerabilities, wounds, and past trauma

As we discussed, these red flags are often concealed in Phase 1: The Hunt by the smoke screen of "love bombs". These overwhelming displays of affection, attention, and adoration are designed to disarm you completely.

Love Bombing: The Initial Assault

"I've never felt this way before about anyone." "You're my soulmate. I knew it the moment we met." "We're so perfect together. We think the same, we like the same things." "I want to know everything about you." "I can't believe I found you. I'm the luckiest man in the world."

Does any of this sound familiar? These aren't just sweet nothings. In the context of narcissistic abuse, they're tactical maneuvers.

Love bombing is the psychological equivalent of a "shock and awe" military campaign. It's designed to overwhelm your defenses, flood your system with feel-good chemicals like dopamine and oxytocin, and create an immediate, intense bond that bypasses your usual radar and vetting process.

During this phase, the Cat studies you meticulously. Every disclosure about your past, every vulnerability you share, every dream you confess becomes *intelligence* for future psychological operations. Your deepest desires are noted not to fulfill them, but to understand what can be dangled before you to establish and maintain control. Your insecurities are cataloged not to handle them with care, but to know exactly what buttons to press when they need to cause you pain.

You're not being loved during this phase. You're being *mapped*.

And yet it feels incredible. What woman doesn't want to be seen, adored, understood, desired so completely? Who doesn't want to believe they've found their perfect match, the one person who finally honors their value for who they truly are?

The intensity feels like intimacy. The attention feels like care. The constant contact feels like connection.

Until it doesn't.

The Gradual Shift From Adoration to Devaluation

Then one day, something changes. Maybe it's subtle at first, like a slightly sharper tone, a dismissive comment, a forgotten promise. Maybe it's more overt, think full-blown rage episode, a disappearance act, a cruel remark about something you hold near and dear.

Whatever form it takes, it's jarring. It contradicts everything you thought you knew about this person and this relationship. It doesn't make a lick of sense.

And that's precisely the point.

This sudden shift creates *cognitive dissonance*—the uncomfortable mental state that occurs when your beliefs don't match your experience. Your brain, desperate to resolve this discomfort, will work overtime to explain away the contradiction.

"He's just stressed out about work." "He didn't mean it that way." "I must have misunderstood." "Everyone has bad days."

The Cat counts on this psychological response. Humans will go to extraordinary lengths to maintain consistency in their beliefs, especially beliefs they've heavily invested in. And by now, you've invested everything in the belief that this person loves you completely.

So, you rationalize. You minimize. You excuse. You blame yourself.

And with that, the battlefield advances inch by inch into the territory of your soul.

The Normalization of Abuse: Redrawing the Battle Map

What follows is a masterclass in psychological manipulation, the gradual normalization of increasingly abusive behavior.

The process follows a fairly predictable pattern:

1. **Boundary violation**: The Cat does something hurtful or disrespectful.

2. **Your reaction**: You express hurt, confusion, or anger.
3. **Invalidation**: The Cat dismisses your feelings as an overreaction.
4. **Gaslighting**: The Cat denies or distorts what actually happened.
5. **Blame-shifting**: The Cat makes their behavior your fault.
6. **Intermittent reinforcement**: Just when you're ready to give up, the loving partner returns briefly.
7. **New normal**: The boundary of acceptable behavior is redrawn to include the previously unacceptable behavior.

Let's see this play out in a real scenario:

The Cat "forgets" your birthday. Not just any birthday, but the one they promised to make special after learning your birthdays were always overlooked as a child.

You express hurt: "I can't believe you forgot my birthday after knowing how important it is to me."

Invalidation: "You're being so dramatic. It's just a day on the calendar."

Gaslighting: "I never *specifically* promised anything for your birthday. You're remembering wrong."

Blame-shifting: "Maybe if you weren't so needy about these things, I wouldn't feel so stressed and could actually remember."

Intermittent reinforcement: Three days later, they show up with a small gift and affection, saying they've been planning it all along but wanted to surprise you.

New normal: Next year, you expect nothing for your birthday and feel grateful for any hint of acknowledgment at all.

Through this process, behaviors that would have been immediate deal-breakers in the beginning of the relationship become your daily reality. The unacceptable becomes acceptable. The abnormal becomes normal.

And more of the battlefield is redrawn to now include *occupied* territory.

Pounce accomplished.

The Battlefield of the Mind

Throughout this gradual shift from romance to warfare, your mind becomes its own battlefield. Cognitive dissonance, that uncomfortable mental state we discussed earlier, becomes your constant companion.

Here's why. You hold two contradictory beliefs simultaneously:

1. "This person loves me deeply and is my soulmate."
2. "This person treats me with contempt and causes me pain."

To resolve this dissonance, you have three options:

1. Change your behavior (i.e., try harder to please them)
2. Change your belief (i.e., accept that they don't truly love you)
3. Add a new belief that bridges the contradiction ("They only hurt me because they're wounded and broken themselves")

Many Beautiful, Intelligent, Tenacious, Courageous, High-value women in abusive relationships choose options 1 and 3. They try harder, walk on eggshells, shower the Cat with gifts, and develop elaborate, savvy explanations for their partner's poor behavior. Anything to avoid option 2, the painful recognition that the love they believed in might not be real after all.

This is how Intelligent, strong women end up accepting treatment for years of their lives that they would never have tolerated initially. The war is not lost, though. In future chapters, we'll discuss strategic escape plans that can lead to victory.

Cat Tactics Decoded

During the love bombing phase, the Cat employs specific tactics that might seem romantic but serve a strategic purpose:

Mirroring: *"We like all the same things! We're so connected!"*

Translation: I'm studying and reflecting back your preferences, values, and mannerisms to create a false sense of compatibility.

Future-faking: *"Next summer, we'll go to Paris." "In five years, we'll have our dream house."*

Translation: I'm creating an imaginary future to keep you invested while I have no intention of following through.

Rushing intimacy: *"Let's move in together. Why wait when we know this is right?"*

Translation: I need to isolate you and increase your dependency before you notice the red flags.

Excessive texting/calling: *"I just wanted to hear your voice again. I can't stop thinking about you."*

Translation: I'm conditioning you with constant contact so I can monitor your activities and establish dominance over your time and attention.

Trauma bonding: *"No one has ever understood my pain like you do."*

Translation: I'm creating an intense emotional connection and empathy through shared vulnerability that will make it harder for you to leave when the abuse begins.

These tactics aren't signs of passion; they're calculated steps in a terroristic campaign to capture your emotional real estate and prepare for the takeover.

Mouse Traps

As this normalization process unfolds, smart women often fall into these predictable traps:

Mistaking apologies for change: Words without actual, consistent change are just tools of manipulation. "I'm sorry" without changed behavior is just a password to get back into your good graces.

The sunk cost fallacy: "I've already invested so much time, resources, and money in this relationship, I can't just walk away now." Ma'am, this trap won "Mouse Trap of the Month" for me every time, as I couldn't fathom walking away from all that time and money, all while spending *more* time and money. This principle will keep you trapped far longer than you need to be.

Trauma-induced loyalty: The intense highs and lows create an addiction so strong that rare moments of peace and affection become more precious than the rubies of your self-worth. You'll willingly endure increasing abuse to experience them.

The messiah complex: "If I just love him enough, I can save him. He'll heal and become the person I know he can be." This trap is particularly alluring for empathetic, caring women.

Recognizing the Battlefield

If you're reading these words and feeling a chill of recognition, know this: The battlefield you're standing on wasn't created by accident. The Cat doesn't "just have anger issues" or "struggle with communication." The deterioration of your once-promising relationship wasn't a mutual failure or an unfortunate drift apart.

It was sinister by design.

Emotional terrorists don't stumble into these patterns; they execute them with precision. The love bombing, the gradual boundary violations, the intermittent reinforcement, the gaslighting—these are tactical maneuvers in a campaign with one main objective: control.

Understanding this truth is both painful and liberating. Painful because it means accepting that what felt like love may have been strategy. Liberating because it means the problem isn't your worthiness, right, or your capacity to be loved.

The problem is that you've been playing a rigged game on a battlefield you believed was covered in a special red carpet—but in actuality, it was many red flags sewn together without a flagpole.

In the next chapter, let's explore how the Cat uses language as a weapon, twisting words and meanings until communication becomes yet another form of control.

But for now, sit with this understanding: The shift from romance to warfare may have been a successful battle, but the war is not over.

Recognizing the battlefield for what it is marks a crucial step toward repossessing your stolen territory.

3

Chapter 3: Decoding the Language of Emotional Terrorism

"God said, 'Let there be light!' So there was light." - Genesis 1:3 ISV

This powerful verse from Genesis reveals a profound truth: Words create worlds.

When God spoke, light separated from darkness. When God named, identity was established. When God declared, reality shifted.

Words have always been vessels of creative power.

But what happens when the power of words is corrupted? What happens when words are twisted, manipulated, and weaponized? What happens when language itself becomes a battlefield in the cat-and-mouse game?

You already know. You've lived it, you're currently living it, or maybe you know someone who's lived it.

You've experienced the disorientation of hearing "I love you" and "You're worthless" from the same mouth. You've felt the confusion of being told "That never happened" about events you clearly remember, or "I never said that" about words you clearly heard with your own two ears. You've endured the cognitive whiplash of "You can't take a joke?!" after a cutting remark left you bleeding.

In the previous chapter, we explored how love gradually transforms into warfare in narcissistic relationships. Now, we'll examine one of the Cat's most potent weapons: Words.

Divine Design vs. Narcissistic Distortion

The Bible tells us in Proverbs 18:21, "Death and life are in the power of the tongue, and those who love it will eat its fruit." This isn't metaphorical or poetic hyperbole. It's literal truth. Words create and destroy. They heal and wound. They build up and tear down.

In God's design, words were meant to:

- Create love, affirmation, and connection between people
- Express and establish truth
- Provide clarity and understanding
- Heal wounds and restore relationships
- Help others overcome challenges and hardships

In the hands of an emotional terrorist, language becomes:

- A tool for confusion and isolation
- A weapon to distort reality
- A means to create doubt and uncertainty
- A method for inflicting wounds no one will find (invisible)
- A vehicle for conditional, manipulative "love"

The contrast couldn't be more clear. What God designed for communion, the narcissist corrupts for control.

And now you, dear mouse, find yourself in a linguistic maze where meanings shift, promises evaporate, and your very perception of reality is called into question.

The Four Horsemen of Linguistic Apocalypse

In narcissistic abuse, four primary language tactics create a perfect storm of confusion and self-doubt in the mouse. Let's decode them one by one.

1. Gaslighting: The Assault on Your Reality

"That never happened." "I never said that." "You're remembering it wrong." "You're too sensitive." "You're crazy."

Sound familiar? These are the common battle cries of gaslighting, a form of psychological manipulation where the abuser makes you question your own memory, perception, and sanity.

The term comes from a 1944 Academy Award-winning film called "Gaslight," where a husband (Cat) deliberately dims the gas lights in their home, then denies that anything has changed when his wife (Mouse) notices. The Cat's goal? To convince her that she's losing her mind.

Gaslighting is lying with a poison cherry on top. It's particularly insidious and worse than lying because it targets your fundamental ability to trust your own thoughts and instincts. Think of it like this: when someone lies, they're typically withholding the truth to escape responsibility, avoid accountability, and erase consequences. The lie has everything to do with the liar's protection, and less to do with damaging or controlling the person being lied to. On the other hand, gaslighting attempts to illuminate false truths about the other person's mental or emotional state. "You're imagining things." "You're just so insecure." "You know your memory is bad." When someone you love and trust repeatedly contradicts your experience and intentionally deceives you with a straight face and a smile, you begin to not only believe the lies, but doubt your ability to use sound judgment.

Proverbs 12:22 tells us: "Lying lips are an abomination to the Lord, but those who act faithfully are his delight." Gaslighting isn't just manipulation—it's a serious spiritual violation that contradicts God's nature and intention for words.

2. Double-speak: The Language of Contradiction

"I'm keeping the debit and credit cards with me because I love you." "I'm only trying to help you improve your money management." "This hurts me more than it hurts you." "I wouldn't have to do this if you weren't so [insert accusation]."

Double-speak occurs when harmful actions are wrapped in the language of love and care. It is designed to mislead the mouse by making the unkind seem kind, and the unacceptable seem acceptable. It creates the cognitive dissonance we spoke about, where abuse masquerades as affection, control disguises itself as concern, and cruelty wears the mask of correction.

This tactic is particularly effective because it targets your desire to believe the best about your partner. You want to believe the Cat loves you, so you accept his framing, even when his actions scream the opposite.

Jesus addressed this kind of contradiction in Matthew 7:15-16: "Beware of false prophets, who come to you in sheep's clothing but inwardly are ravenous wolves. You will recognize them by their fruits."

The fruits—the actual impact of the Cat's words and actions—reveal the truth behind the double-speak. Real love will never leave you feeling worthless. Real care will never leave you walking on eggshells. Real concern will never diminish your sense of self.

3. Word Salad: The Fog of Confusion

Have you ever asked a simple question and received a response so convoluted, so circular, so packed with tangents and false accusations that you forgot what you asked in the first place? Honey, that's word salad—a verbal technique designed to confuse, exhaust, and ultimately silence you. No, you are not afraid to speak your mind, make your point, or share your heart. That's what Intelligent, High-value women do. You have more to say, and what's on your mind is important. But by the time this weapon finishes with you, you have zero energy left to do anything else but wave a white flag.

Word salad often includes:

· Rapid topic changes
· Circular reasoning

· Illogical conclusions
· Projection of their actions onto you
· Victim-blaming
· Previously settled grievances
· Extreme or loud emotional displays

The goal is simple: to create such mental and emotional torment that you abandon your original point just to make the conversation stop.

If you swallow the effects of *word salad* whole, prepare for the indigestion of indictment. "We can never get anywhere because you always bail on the conversation." "See, this is why I don't open up to you." "You only want to hear your voice in this relationship!" Unlike divine communication characterized by clarity and simplicity, the Cat will consistently use rotten word salad on the battlefield of emotional terrorism.

4. Selective Memory: The Convenient Amnesiac

"We never agreed to that." "I've always supported your career." "I've never once raised my voice at you." "I've been nothing but faithful."

Selective memory involves the strategic remembering or forgetting of events to serve the narcissist's narrative. Positive interactions are magnified, while negative ones are erased. Promises are "forgotten" when inconvenient, then all of a sudden "remembered" differently when challenged.

You'll notice in the examples shared that the root of selective memory typically involves one particular part of speech: adverbs. Oh, the battle of the adverbs "always" and "never". The Cat will use these two particular adverbs to justify *forgetting* or *remembering* the narrative that suits them best. For example, "always" will be weaponized against holding the Cat accountable to promises made. "I didn't say 'always'. You want me to be perfect when you're not even perfect." "Never" will be weaponized against any inconsequential omissions and errors. "You said I would do it on Tuesday—wrong! I never said a day. Now who's the liar?!"

This tactic is particularly effective because it creates a false history of the relationship where the Cat is always loving, always supportive, always right.

Your contradicting memories are dismissed as faulty, biased, or malicious.

Proverbs 14:5 speaks to this: "A faithful witness does not lie, but a false witness breathes out lies." The selective memory of the narcissist is not accidental forgetfulness, nor is it a sign that he has fallen victim to a serious brain issue. It's a deliberate falsification of history that breathes life into their manipulation and control.

The Cumulative Impact: Linguistic Terrorism

These four tactics—gaslighting, double-speak, word salad, and selective memory—rarely operate in isolation. They work together in toxic harmony, reinforcing each other in a comprehensive assault on your perception of reality.

Over time, this linguistic terrorism creates:

1. **Chronic self-doubt**: You stop trusting your own perceptions and memories.
2. **Cognitive fog**: Your thinking becomes clouded and confused.
3. **Emotional exhaustion**: You're too tired to fight for the truth anymore.
4. **Silence**: You stop expressing your needs, concerns, or observations to avoid conflict.
5. **Isolation**: You withdraw from others who might catch on to your relationship reality.

The result is a profound disconnection from yourself, from others, and from God's truth. You become a stranger in your own life, unable to trust the very faculties God gave you to navigate the world.

And that's exactly what the Cat wants.

Cat Tactics Decoded

Let's examine some specific verbal tactics the Cat employs and decode their true meaning:

"You're too sensitive."

Translation: Your emotional responses are inconvenient to me, so I'm invalidating them rather than taking responsibility for my hurtful behavior.

"If you really loved me, you wouldn't question me/complain/give me a hard time."

Translation: I'm using your love as a weapon against you to avoid accountability and maintain control.

"I was just joking. Can't you take a joke?"

Translation: I want the freedom to hurt you without consequences, and I'll make you feel defective for having a normal reaction.

"You're remembering it wrong. That's not what happened."

Translation: My version of reality is the only acceptable one, and I'll make you doubt your own mind rather than admit the truth.

"After everything I've done for you, this is how you repay me?"

Translation: I keep a ledger of my "good deeds" to use as ammunition when you express legitimate needs or concerns.

"You're just like your mother/father/ex."

Translation: I'm using your deepest insecurities, fears, or past trauma against you to shut down this conversation.

"No one else would put up with you."

Translation: I need to destroy your sense of worth so you won't realize you deserve better and leave me.

"I never said that. You're making things up again."

Translation: I refuse to be held accountable for my words, and I'll make you question your sanity rather than admit what I said.

These tactics aren't random cruelty. They're calculated maneuvers in the Cat's campaign to maintain dominance through linguistic control.

Mouse Traps

Here are common pitfalls that can keep smart women trapped in this linguistic maze:

Seeking logical consistency: Trying to make sense of contradictory statements keeps you mentally bogged down with nonsense. Not everything deserves the dignity of your analysis.

Believing words over patterns: Focusing on what they say rather than the consistent patterns of their behavior keeps you hoping for change that never comes.

Accepting their definitions: Allowing them to re-define what love, respect, or abuse means creates a rigged game where the rules constantly change to your disadvantage.

Abandoning truth to keep peace: Surrendering your reality to avoid conflict only emboldens the Cat to push further into your soul's territory.

Isolating from outside perspectives: Cutting off people who might validate your perception leaves you with the Cat's distorted reality as a frame of reference.

Repossess Your Language

"No weapon formed against you shall prosper" (Isaiah 54:17). This includes weapons forged from twisted words and manipulated meanings.

Here are some initial steps toward linguistic liberation:

1. **Keep a private journal**. Document conversations, incidents, and feelings where you felt stuck in the linguistic maze. This creates an external record that can minimize the effects of gaslighting.
2. **Find a reality anchor**. Identify at least one person who can provide perspective and validation. Therapists, support groups, or trusted friends can serve this role.
3. **Practice truth statements**. Simple declarations like "That happened" or "I know what I experienced" can strengthen your connection to reality.

4. **Agree with divine truth**. God's Word provides an unchanging standard against which all other words can be measured. Immerse yourself in scripture to recalibrate your discernment.
5. **Name the tactics**. When you can identify "That's gaslighting" or "That's word salad," the tactics will lose some of their impact over you.
6. **Reduce JADE (Justify, Argue, Defend, Explain)**. The more you JADE, the more kibble you feed the Cat for manipulation. Simple, direct statements require less emotional investment.
7. **Embrace silence**. Sometimes the most powerful response is no response. Not every accusation deserves a defense, not every question an answer.

Remember the words of Jesus in John 8:32: "And you will know the truth, and the truth will set you free." Your journey toward freedom begins with repossessing your right to trust your judgment, name your own experiences, and speak the truth.

The Cat has used language as a weapon against you, but words were God's idea first. Words were designed to create, not destroy; to connect, not isolate; to clarify, not confuse. Even though the Cat tries to pervert the original design of language, know that your voice still matters. And no amount of linguistic terrorism can change that fundamental truth.

In the next chapter, we'll explore why smart women often stay in these relationships longer than one might expect, and address the false narratives we tell and sell ourselves.

But for now, hold fast to this: God is the author of truth, and no twisted words can separate you from His divine reality and love.

4

Chapter 4: The People-Pleasing Prison: When Survival Becomes Self-Destructive

"Fear of man will prove to be a snare, but whoever trusts in the Lord is kept safe."
– Proverbs 29:25 NIV

Sis, you're too good. You've perfected the art of reading the room. You can sense tension before it erupts, anticipate needs before they're expressed, and adjust your personality to match whatever the situation requires. You pride yourself on being easy-going, accommodating, and conflict-free. People often tell you how "sweet" and "agreeable" you are.

But underneath this carefully crafted exterior, you're exhausted. You've lost touch with your own preferences, your own needs, your own voice. You say yes when you mean no, smile when you want to cry, and agree when you want to argue. You've become so skilled at being what others want you to be that you've forgotten who you actually are.

This is the people-pleasing prison, and if you're reading this book, chances are you've been living in it for a long time.

I was your jailmate, the president of the People-Pleasers Club. See, what started as a survival strategy born from childhood sexual abuse became a way of life that slowly eroded my sense of self and self-worth. Contorting myself into unrecognizable shapes for others earned me access to love, acceptance, connection—or so I thought.

People-pleasing isn't kindness. It's not generosity, selflessness, or Christ-like love. It's a trauma response, a defense mechanism, and often a setup for the very abuse you're trying to avoid. Understanding this distinction is crucial because it's the difference between genuine care for others and self-destructive behavior disguised as virtue.

In this chapter, we'll explore the roots of people-pleasing, how it functions as both a survival strategy and a mouse trap in toxic relationships, and the devastating impact it has on your identity and self-worth. Most importantly, we'll begin to understand how people-pleasing actually makes you a target in the cat-and-mouse game.

The Roots of People-Pleasing

People-pleasing doesn't develop in a vacuum. It's a learned behavior that typically originates in childhood when a young person discovers that their safety, love, or acceptance depends on keeping others happy. Understanding where your people-pleasing patterns began is essential for healing them.

Common Origins of People-Pleasing:

Conditional love in childhood. If you learned that love was contingent on your behavior, performance, or ability to keep those you truly love happy, you developed people-pleasing as a survival strategy. Children who experience conditional love learn that their worth is tied to their ability to please others.

Emotional parentification. If you were responsible for managing your parents' emotions, keeping the peace in your family, or taking care of others' needs before your own, you learned that your value came from your caretaking abilities.

Punishment for authentic expression. If you were criticized, rejected, or punished for expressing your true thoughts, feelings, or needs, you learned that authenticity was dangerous and that safety came from suppression and being agreeable.

Chaotic or unpredictable environments. If you grew up in an environment where you never knew what mood someone would be in or what would trigger their anger, you developed hyper-vigilance and people-pleasing as ways to create predictability and safety.

Religious or cultural conditioning. Some religious or cultural environments teach that selflessness, submission, and putting others first are the highest virtues, without teaching healthy boundaries or self-care. This can create people-pleasing patterns disguised as spiritual maturity.

Trauma and abuse. Any form of childhood trauma or abuse can create people-pleasing patterns as the child learns that their survival depends on keeping their abuser calm and happy.

The People-Pleasing Mindset:

People-pleasing is driven by several core beliefs that feel true but are actually distortions:

- "My worth depends on how others feel about me."
- "If I can just be good enough, I'll be safe and loved."
- "Other people's needs are more important than mine."
- "Conflict is dangerous and must be avoided at all costs."
- "I'm responsible for other people's emotions and reactions."
- "If someone is upset with me, I must have done something wrong."
- "Saying no makes me selfish and bad."

These beliefs create a worldview where your value is entirely external; you exist to serve others' needs, and your own thoughts, feelings, and needs are irrelevant or dangerous to express.

People-Pleasing as Self-Preservation

In the context of the Cat-and-mouse game, people-pleasing serves as a defense mechanism. When you're dealing with someone who is unpredictable, controlling, or abusive, people-pleasing can feel like your only option for survival. Understanding this helps you have compassion for yourself while also recognizing why this strategy ultimately fails.

How People-Pleasing Functions as Defense:

Conflict avoidance. If you can anticipate the Cat's needs and meet them before they become demands, you might avoid their anger, criticism, or punishment. People-pleasing becomes a way to stay under the radar and prevent explosive reactions.

Control through compliance. When you feel powerless in a relationship, people-pleasing can give you a sense of control. If you can just be perfect enough, agreeable enough, helpful enough, maybe you can control their behavior and keep yourself safe.

Love insurance. People-pleasing can feel like insurance against abandonment. If you're always giving, always accommodating, always putting their needs first, surely they won't leave you, right? Wrong. Your value becomes tied to your usefulness, and nothing could be farther from the truth.

Identity protection. When someone is constantly criticizing or attacking your character, people-pleasing can feel like a way to prove them wrong. If you can just be good enough, maybe they'll stop telling you that you're selfish, difficult, problematic, or too hard to love.

Emotional regulation. If you've accepted responsibility for managing someone else's emotions, people-pleasing becomes a way to keep their mood stable, which in turn keeps your environment stable and predictable.

Why People-Pleasing Fails as a Strategy:

The tragic irony of people-pleasing is that it often creates the very problems it's designed to solve:

It attracts takers. Did you know that people-pleasing has a scent? People who are selfish, manipulative, or abusive are drawn to people-pleasers because they provide easy targets for exploitation and manipulation.

It enables bad behavior. When you consistently accommodate unreasonable demands, absorb someone's emotions, and avoid addressing problems, you're actually *enabling* and *reinforcing* their problematic behavior. Why would they ever change?

It creates resentment. While you're busy meeting everyone else's needs, your own needs go unmet. This creates a buildup of resentment that eventually explodes or implodes, often damaging the very relationships you were trying to protect.

It prevents authentic connection. Relationships built on people-pleasing are relationships with a false self. The other person doesn't actually know you; they know the version of you that you think they want to see.

It teaches dishonor. People-pleasing communicates to others that you don't value yourself, your time, or your needs. This often leads others to treat you with the same lack of respect that you're showing yourself. You become their worst teacher.

The Cat's Exploitation of People-Pleasing

Emotional terrorists have an uncanny ability to identify people-pleasers. Your people-pleasing patterns make you an ideal target because they signal that you're willing to sacrifice your own needs for someone else's comfort, that you're unlikely to enforce boundaries, and that you'll work hard to avoid conflict at all costs—an ideal mouse for the cat-and-mouse game.

How the Cat Exploits People-Pleasing:

Love-bombing the people-pleaser. The Cat recognizes your people-pleasing patterns and initially rewards them with excessive attention, affection, and praise. They make you feel like your accommodating nature is your greatest asset and that they've finally found someone who truly understands them.

Escalating demands. Once the Cat has established that you're willing to please them, they begin escalating their demands. What started as small accommodations becomes major sacrifices. "We're together all the time anyway, maybe I should just move in with you." Each time you comply, the bar gets higher.

Punishment for boundaries. When you *occasionally* try to assert a boundary or express a need, the Cat responds with anger, withdrawal, or punishment.

This reinforces your belief that people-pleasing is safer than authenticity.

Creating impossible standards. The Cat creates standards that are impossible to meet, ensuring that you're always falling short. No matter how much you give, it's never enough.

Weaponizing your compassion. The Cat learns to use your empathy and compassion against you. They present themselves as victims, create crises that require your help, or manipulate your emotions to get what they want.

Isolating you from support. The Cat gradually isolates you from people who might point out the unhealthy dynamics or encourage you to prioritize your own needs. They want to be your only voice of validation and feedback.

The Damage to Self-Esteem and Identity

Life in a people-pleasing prison causes profound damage to your sense of self. When your entire identity hinges on the yo-yo of meeting others' needs and avoiding their displeasure, you lose touch with your own God-given identity.

How People-Pleasing Damages Self-Esteem:

External validation dependency. When your worth depends on others' approval, your self-esteem becomes completely external. You have no internal sense of value, which makes you vulnerable to the Cat's manipulation and abuse.

Chronic self-neglect. People-pleasing requires you to consistently ignore your own needs, feelings, and desires. Over time, this creates a pattern of self-neglect that becomes so automatic you don't even notice it anymore.

Imposter syndrome. Because you're constantly performing a *version* of yourself designed to please others, you develop a sense that you're not authentic, that people wouldn't like the "real" you, and that you're somehow a fraud who's fooling everyone.

How People-Pleasing Erodes Identity:

Suppressed emotions. Is it hard for you to cry or have a hearty laugh out loud? People-pleasing requires you to suppress any emotions that might be inconvenient for others. Over time, you may lose the ability to identify and express your authentic feelings.

Silenced voice. When you consistently prioritize others' opinions over your own, your internal and external voice becomes weaker and weaker. Your identity as one with the power of life and death in your voice becomes compromised.

Blurred boundaries. People-pleasing erodes your sense of where you end and others begin. You may take responsibility for others' emotions while neglecting your own, or feel guilty for having needs that differ from someone else's.

Role confusion. When your identity becomes organized around being helpful, accommodating, and agreeable, you lose sight of how powerful you are outside of these roles. Your sense of self becomes dependent on your function rather than your inherent worth.

The People-Pleasing Paradox

You mean well, but one of the most painful aspects of people-pleasing is that it often creates the very outcomes you're trying to avoid. This paradox keeps you trapped in cycles of increasing self-sacrifice with diminishing returns. What does this look like? Let's decode.

The Paradox in Action:

You please to avoid rejection, but people-pleasing attracts people who will ultimately reject the real you. When you build relationships on people-pleasing, you're building them on a false foundation. Eventually, either you'll burn out from the performance, or they'll grow bored and lose interest when they realize you only have one play to offer—pleasing. Even the most manipulative Cat can grow weary from always winning every round.

You please to avoid conflict, but people-pleasing creates more conflict. When you don't address issues directly, do they disappear? No, they fester. Your resentment builds, their expectations increase, and eventually the conflict you were avoiding becomes unavoidable towards a boiling point.

You please to feel valued, but people-pleasing communicates that you don't value yourself. When you consistently put others' needs before your own, you're teaching them that your needs don't matter—even if they pretend otherwise. Isn't it time to stop settling for fake gratitude and platitudes?

You please to maintain control, but people-pleasing gives your power away. While people-pleasing can feel like a way to influence others' behavior, it actually hands control of your life over to other people's moods, needs, and demands.

You please to be loved, but people-pleasing prevents authentic love. I get it. When you're in a love drought, even a sprinkle of faux love waters your dry, broken soul. But you deserve to be drenched, sis. Real love requires knowing and accepting someone for who they truly are. If you're always performing, always accommodating, always hiding your true self, you can't be truly known *or* truly loved.

Cat Tactics Decoded

The Appreciation Manipulation: The Cat showers you with praise for your accommodating nature, making you feel like your people-pleasing works wonders and is your most valuable quality. Sweet manipulation like "You're so understanding, you get me" or "I love how easy-going you are" feeds your ego and strokes your esteem.

The Guilt Trip: When you occasionally try to assert a boundary or express a need, the Cat responds with guilt trips designed to pull you back into people-pleasing mode. They might say things like "I thought you cared about me, you're just like everybody else" or "You're being so selfish" to manipulate you back into compliance.

The Moving Goalpost: The Cat constantly changes their expectations and demands, ensuring that no amount of people-pleasing is ever enough—and neither are you. Just when you think you've finally pleased them, they find something new to be dissatisfied about.

Mouse Traps

The Kindness Trap: You believe that people-pleasing is the same as being kind or loving. Remember, true kindness sometimes requires saying no, setting boundaries, and refusing to enable bad behavior.

The Martyrdom Trap: You take *pride* in your self-sacrifice and see it as evidence of your moral superiority. This keeps you trapped in people-pleasing patterns because giving them up would require giving up your identity as the "good" person who always puts others first.

The Fear Trap: You're so afraid of conflict, rejection, disapproval, or abandonment that you'll do anything to avoid these experiences, even if it means sacrificing your authentic self. This fear keeps you trapped in people-pleasing patterns that actually increase the likelihood of these outcomes.

Breaking Free from People-Pleasing

Recognizing people-pleasing patterns is the first step toward freedom, but breaking free requires intentional effort and practice. It means learning to tolerate the discomfort of others' displeasure.

Baby Steps Toward Freedom:

Identify your people-pleasing triggers. What situations, people, or emotions trigger your people-pleasing responses? Awareness is the first step toward change.

Know the power of no. Start small with low-stakes situations and gradually work up to more challenging scenarios. Saying, "No, I can't go, but thanks for asking" is sufficient. You don't need to say anything else. Less is more.

Reconnect with your preferences. Spend time figuring out what you actually like, want, and need. This may require experimentation and patience as you rediscover your authentic self.

Set and enforce boundaries. In Chapter 16, we'll discuss *Courageous boundaries*. Learning to communicate your limits clearly and following through with consequences when they're violated is totally possible.

Tolerate others' displeasure. Practice sitting with the discomfort of knowing someone is upset with you without immediately rushing to fix it or apologize.

Breaking free from people-pleasing isn't about becoming selfish or uncaring. You don't have to become *that* person to honor yourself authentically. It's about learning to care for others from a place of choice rather than confusion or compulsion, from strength rather than fear or performance.

In the next chapter, we'll explore how the Cat uses intermittent reinforcement to create addiction-like bonds that keep you trapped in the cycle of abuse. We'll discover how the unpredictable nature of their affection creates a powerful psychological hook that's designed to keep you coming back for more, even when you know better.

For now, remember: your worth is not determined by your ability to please others. You are valuable simply because you exist, not because you make others happy.

"Am I now trying to win the approval of human beings, or of God? Or am I trying to please people? If I were still trying to please people, I would not be a servant of Christ." – Galatians 1:10

5

Chapter 5: The Intelligent Woman's Blind Spot

"Let no one deceive you with empty words..." - Ephesians 5:6 NIV

Intelligent. The "I" in B.I.T.C.H. It's such a gift, isn't it?

The ability to analyze, strategize, problem-solve, and understand complex situations. The capacity to learn quickly, adapt, and find creative solutions. The power to see patterns, make connections, and anticipate outcomes.

But what happens when this divine gift—this Beautiful, powerful part of how you were fearfully and wonderfully made—becomes the very thing that keeps you trapped in the Cat-and-mouse game?

It sounds kind of counterintuitive, doesn't it? Shouldn't intelligence be your ticket out? Shouldn't your brilliant mind recognize the patterns of abuse, calculate the cost-benefit analysis of staying, and logically conclude it's time to leave?

And yet, here you are. There I was. Smart, capable, accomplished—and seemingly stuck. We are not alone.

In her groundbreaking work, *"Smart, Successful & Abused: The Unspoken Problem of Domestic Violence and High-Achieving Women,"* neuroscientist Dr. Angela Mailis (2019) documents how highly Intelligent, educated women often stay in abusive relationships longer than their counterparts based on ten key factors: low self-esteem, codependency, fear of being alone, lack of experience, shame, external pressures, excess empathy, people-pleasing, concern for the welfare of the children, and money troubles. The very cognitive abilities that serve you so well in corporate offices, boardrooms, hospitals, universities, and courts of law have become your blind spot.

In Psalm 139:14, David writes, "I praise you because I am fearfully and wonderfully made; your works are wonderful, I know that full well." This verse reminds us that every aspect of your being, including your mind, was crafted with divine intention and purpose. Your intelligence isn't a flaw; it's a gift from God meant to serve you.

So how has this gift been turned against you? How has the Cat managed to transform one of your greatest strengths into your most vulnerable weakness?

Let's explore the psychological mechanisms at play and decode the blind spots that keep smart women trapped in the game longer than they should be.

The Weaponization of Wisdom

In Genesis 1:27, we learn that "God created mankind in his own image." This means your intelligence—your capacity for wisdom, discernment, and understanding—reflects the divine image. It's part of your soul's DNA.

But the Cat has studied you. Observed you. Mapped your intellectual terrain with predatory precision. And in doing so, he's identified exactly how to use your God-given intelligence against you.

Here's how it typically unfolds:

1. Cognitive Biases: The Mind's Blind Spots

Your brain is a marvel of creation that comes with *shortcut* features called cognitive biases, which help you process information quickly and efficiently. But sometimes these biases can lead you astray. In abusive relationships, these particular biases often become mouse traps:

Confirmation Bias: You selectively gather and interpret information that confirms what you *want* to believe about the relationship. You may notice this in your keyword searches on Google, or by consistently seeking advice from that friend who thinks like you. With this bias, you magnify the good times ("See? He can be so loving!"), and minimize the bad ones ("It wasn't really that serious.").

Normalcy Bias: A form of denial, you have difficulty believing that the relationship is as bad as it is. You struggle to believe that something so outside your normal experience could be happening to you. "I am not in an abusive relationship. Abuse happens to other women, not educated women like me."

Optimism Bias: You overestimate the likelihood of positive outcomes and underestimate negative ones. Remember emotional terrorism's slot machine in Chapter 1? "He'll change. Next time will be different. We just need to get through this rough patch."

Authority Bias: If the Cat has credentials, status, influence, or is highly respected in the community, you give their perspective more weight than it deserves. "He's a deacon at church." "He's a city councilman. Everyone loves to be around him. Maybe I am the problem."

These biases aren't character flaws. They're universal human tendencies. But in the context of narcissistic abuse, they become the first layer of the intelligent woman's blind spot.

2. Trauma Bonding: The Biochemical Trap

Your brain doesn't just process information; it processes chemicals. And in abusive relationships, it processes a lot of them.

Trauma bonding occurs when the abuse creates a biochemical addiction cycle. As we discussed in Chapter 2, during periods of abuse, your body floods with stress hormones like cortisol and adrenaline. When the abuse temporarily stops, you experience relief and a surge of dopamine and oxytocin, the same chemicals released during positive bonding experiences.

This creates a powerful addiction cycle that has nothing to do with your intelligence and everything to do with your neurobiology. Your brilliant mind works overtime to justify this biochemical attachment, creating elaborate explanations for why you need to stay. Your intelligence is used to strategize how to reclaim the high versus analyzing why you're still in the game.

It's not weakness. It's not stupidity. It's a physiological response to trauma that can happen to anyone, regardless of IQ.

3. Savior Complex: The Distorted Mission

Many intelligent women, especially those with faith backgrounds, develop what psychologists call a "Savior complex" in abusive relationships. You believe it's your divine mission to heal, fix, or save your abuser.

This complex often has roots in a misinterpretation of scripture. Yes, God calls us to love sacrificially. Yes, Jesus modeled servant leadership. But nowhere does God ask you to sacrifice your safety, dignity, or emotional health on the altar of someone's abuse.

Proverbs 14:7 advises, "Stay away from a fool, for you will not find knowledge on their lips." Sometimes the most godly thing you can do is walk away from someone who refuses wisdom and persists in foolishness.

Your intelligence, combined with your compassion, creates a dangerous cocktail of rationalization: "If I just love him enough... If I just understand him better... If I just find the right approach... I can help him heal."

Your intellectual juices are struggling to swim upstream, and it's not a divine assignment. It's a trap.

4. Sunk Cost Fallacy: The Logical Illusion

As discussed in Chapter 2 (are you picking up on the reinforcements?), the sunk cost fallacy is flawed "intelligence" where you continue investing in something because of what you've already invested, not because you have any evidence of future returns. It's the "I've already put 5 years into this relationship, I can't leave him now!" mentality.

Smart women are particularly vulnerable to this fallacy because:

1. We value commitment and follow-through.
2. We've likely invested significantly in the relationship (time, money, energy).
3. We're good at delayed gratification.
4. We believe in working through problems.
5. Our optimism and faith metrics are through the roof.

Don't miss this. The sunk cost fallacy ignores a fundamental truth: You can't recover time, energy, or love already spent. The only relevant question is whether staying will yield better or worse outcomes than leaving, regardless of what you've already invested.

Ecclesiastes 3:6 NIV reminds us there is "a time to search and a time to give up, a time to keep and a time to throw away." Godly intelligence includes knowing when to cut your losses, not just when to suffer in perseverance.

The Intelligence Paradox

So, here's the cruel irony, sis: the smarter you are, the more elaborate your rationalizations become. Your brilliant mind constructs increasingly complex explanations for the Cat's behavior, and your excuses for his actions become sexier and sexier:

"His childhood trauma explains his anger issues." "His narcissistic tendencies stem from the deep insecurity no one helped him address." "His controlling behavior is just his love language discombobulated." "His emotional volatility is due to undiagnosed mental health issues." "He's displacing the effects of a disjointed relationship with his mother/father onto me."

Now, some of your explanations might even be accurate. But here's what your intelligence hasn't yet grasped: *Understanding the origins of abuse doesn't obligate you to endure it.*

You can understand why someone behaves abusively while still refusing to be their victim. You can acknowledge their woundedness with compassion without allowing them to wound you. You can pray for their healing from a safe distance.

As Proverbs 4:23 instructs, "Above all else, guard your heart, for everything you do flows from it." This isn't selfish; it's stewardship of the life God gave you.

Cat Tactics Decoded

In the realm of intellectual manipulation, the Cat employs specific tactics designed to exploit your intelligence. Let's decode them:

Intellectual Gaslighting: "You're overthinking this. You always make everything so complicated."

Translation: Your analytical abilities threaten my control, so I'm invalidating your thought process rather than engaging with your legitimate concerns.

Complexity Creation: "It's not that simple. There are so many factors at play here that you're not considering."

Translation: I'm deliberately over-complicating the situation to exhaust your mental resources and make you doubt your own analysis.

Moving the Intellectual Goalposts: "That's not what I meant. You're smart enough to understand the nuance of what I was saying."

Translation: I'm using your desire to deeply understand as a way to never be pinned down to any statement or commitment.

Credentialing: "With my background/education/experience, I have a better perspective on this than you do."

Translation: I'm using institutional authority or specialized knowledge to override your valid perceptions and experiences.

Philosophical Smoke Screens: "What is truth, really? What is an apology? Isn't everything subjective? Who can say what's right or wrong?"

Translation: I'm using pseudo-intellectual relativism to avoid accountability for a clear violation of respect and loyalty.

Weaponized Vulnerability: "I'm sharing my deepest trauma with you because you're the only one who truly understands me."

Translation: I'm exploiting your intelligence-linked empathy by making you feel uniquely qualified to help me, creating a responsibility bond that's hard to break.

Intellectual Flattery: "You're so smart. That's why I need you. I love a woman with brains. No one else challenges me like you do."

Translation: I'm praising your intelligence to keep you invested in a relationship that primarily serves my needs.

Research Assignment: "If you really want to understand what I'm saying, read/watch these books/articles/studies/websites/videos."

Translation: I know how much you like an intellectual challenge—to prove me wrong. So I'm outsourcing the work of explaining my behavior to external sources, keeping you busy researching rather than leaving.

These tactics are calculated exploitations of your intellectual strengths, designed to keep you engaged in solving an unsolvable puzzle. You can't single-handedly make an abusive relationship healthy.

Mouse Traps

Even with your remarkable intelligence, there are specific *intellectual* mouse traps that can keep you caught in the game:

The Explanation Addiction: You believe that if you can just understand why the Cat behaves abusively, you can solve the problem. Or, if you could find a way to adequately explain why the Cat's behavior is abusive, he will see the light and want to change. But understanding the why rarely changes the what. Explanation for you becomes a substitute for action.

The Exceptional Woman Fallacy: "Other women might need to leave abusive partners, but I'm smart enough to navigate this." This intellectual *pride* becomes a prison, keeping you trying to solve a problem the Cat can't and refuses to see.

The Data Collection Loop: You keep gathering more information, more evidence/receipts, more perspective before making a decision. But no amount of data will create perfect certainty. At some point, wisdom requires action despite incomplete information.

The Intellectual Isolation: You stop sharing your relationship struggles with others because "no one would understand the complexity of our situation." This cuts you off from outside perspectives that might clarify what your too-close analysis cannot see.

The Redemption Narrative: Your intelligence crafts a Beautiful story where suffering leads to transformation. You imagine the lives that will be touched by your and the Cat's testimony on the other side of this darkness. You're not just in an abusive relationship; you're on a hero's journey. This narrative keeps you enduring what God never asked you to endure.

The False Equivalence: Your nuanced thinking sees how you've made mistakes too, creating a false equivalence between your imperfections and their abuse. "We've both hurt each other" becomes the rationalization for staying.

The Intellectual Humility Trap: You're smart enough to know you don't know everything, which the Cat exploits by making you doubt even your clearest perceptions. "Maybe I'm missing something" becomes the thought that keeps you stuck.

These traps do not exploit your weaknesses but definitely your strengths— your analytical depth, your nuanced thinking, your intellectual humility, your meaning-making abilities. They transform your cognitive gifts into cognitive chains.

Repossess Your God-Given Intelligence

Ephesians 2:10 reminds us, "For we are God's handiwork, created in Christ Jesus to do good works, which God prepared in advance for us to do." Your intelligence is part of that divine handiwork, designed for your flourishing, not your captivity.

Here are steps toward reclaiming your intellectual sovereignty:

1. **Recognize the paradox**: Acknowledge that in this specific context, your intelligence may be working against you, not for you. This isn't a permanent state, but a contextual one.
2. **Seek outside perspective**: Find a therapist, counselor, or support group specifically trained in abuse dynamics. External validation can help recalibrate your normalized perception.
3. **Simplify the question**: Instead of "Why does he do this?", ask "Is this behavior acceptable to me?" Instead of "How can I fix this?", ask "Should I be the one trying to fix this?"
4. **Trust your body**: Your physical and emotional responses often recognize

danger before your intellect does. If you feel afraid, anxious, or like you're walking on eggshells, listen to that intuition.

5. **Set a decision timeline**: Your brilliant mind can analyze forever (LOL). Set a specific time frame for making a decision about the relationship to avoid the endless data collection loop.

6. **Challenge your narratives**: Examine the stories you tell yourself about why you stay. Are they truly aligned with God's vision for your life and relationships?

7. **Embrace intellectual humility**: True wisdom includes knowing the boundaries of your understanding. You cannot fully comprehend, predict, or control another person's choices.

8. **Reframe intelligence**: Real intelligence isn't just fixing and problem-solving; it's also problem-recognition, knowing when a situation is fundamentally broken, not just temporarily challenged.

Remember Jeremiah 29:11: "'For I know the plans I have for you,' declares the LORD, 'plans to prosper you and not to harm you, plans to give you hope and a future.'" God's plan for you includes relationships that honor your whole being—which includes your magnificent mind.

Your intelligence isn't a design flaw in God's creation, it's a feature. A Beautiful, powerful aspect of being made in His image. The problem isn't your intelligence itself but how it's been hijacked in the context of abuse.

Proverbs 31 describes a woman of noble character whose qualities include strength, wisdom, and discernment. "[She] speaks with wisdom, and faithful instruction is on her tongue." This is God's vision for your intellectual gifts—not that they would keep you trapped, but that they would guide you toward freedom, purpose, and flourishing.

The Cat has temporarily turned your intelligence against you. But that same intelligence, realigned with divine wisdom, will ultimately be your path to freedom.

In the next section, we'll shift our focus from understanding the game to understanding the Cat, exploring the anatomy of narcissistic traits and behavior patterns.

But for now, hold fast to this truth: You were fearfully and wonderfully made—intelligence and all. And no amount of manipulation can change the divine intention behind your creation.

II

SECTION II: UNDERSTANDING THE CAT

6

Chapter 6: The Anatomy of a Narcissist

"Pride disgusts the Lord." - Proverbs 16:5 TLB

Have you ever wondered what makes the Cat tick?

What internal machinery drives the person that causes you so much pain? What invisible wounds lie beneath their polished, likable exterior?

Understanding the inner workings of a strongly narcissistic person isn't about excusing their behavior. It's about arming yourself with knowledge. And while narcissism is more extensive than what one book can cover, there are some interesting "purrks" to knowing what can lie deep within the Cat's purr. As Solomon wrote in Proverbs 24:5, "The wise prevail through great power, and those who have knowledge muster their strength." Your knowledge is power. Your understanding is strength.

So, let's put in some reps! Shall we?

The Cat operates from a fundamentally different reality than you do. While you may navigate the world with normal human vulnerabilities, insecurities, empathy, and a capacity for genuine connection, the narcissist exists in a carefully constructed alternate universe where they are the sun, and everyone else merely rotates in their orbit.

Let's pull back the curtain and examine what truly lies beneath the surface of the person who has turned your life into an emotional and psychological battlefield.

The Narcissistic Worldview: Core Beliefs and Perceptions

At the heart of narcissistic personality lies a set of deeply held beliefs about themselves and the world:

"*I am special and unique.*" Not in the healthy way we're all unique creations of God, but in a grandiose sense that places them above normal human limitations and rules.

"*I deserve special treatment.*" The narcissist genuinely believes that ordinary standards don't apply to them. Their time is more valuable, their needs more pressing, their assumptions and opinions more correct.

"*Others exist to serve my needs.*" People aren't fully human to the narcissist; they're objects, extensions, means, or tools. This includes you.

"*Vulnerability is weakness.*" Any admission of fault, insecurity, or responsibility is intolerable and must be avoided at all costs.

"*Life is a zero-sum game.*" If someone else wins, the narcissist loses. If someone else receives praise, their light is diminished.

These aren't intentional, conscious thoughts. They're the invisible operating system running beneath every interaction, every decision, and every emotional response the Cat has. They're as automatic and unquestioned as breathing and blinking.

Proverbs 16:18 tells us that "Pride goes before destruction, a haughty spirit before a fall." The narcissist's worldview is built on the shakiest of foundations: pride that cannot tolerate even the slightest crack or weakness.

The Wounded Core: Origins of Narcissistic Patterns

Contrary to popular belief, narcissism isn't born from excessive childhood praise or "too much self-esteem." It's actually the opposite. Narcissistic patterns typically develop from profound early wounds to the child's developing Self (Ronningstam, 2005).

Some narcissists experienced childhood trauma, neglect, or abuse. They never felt love and validation from the parent they considered to be their hero. Others had parents who used them as extensions of themselves, valuing them only for achievements or appearances. Still others had caregivers who taught them that love is both conditional and inconsistent.

Research also reveals a significant genetic component to narcissistic patterns. Twin studies have consistently shown that narcissistic personality traits are amongst the most heritable of all personality disorders, with heritability estimates as high as 79% (Torgersen et al., 2012). This means that narcissism can travel through bloodlines, and pass from one generation to the next through genetic inheritance. A child may be born with a biological predisposition toward narcissistic traits long before environmental factors come into play. This genetic vulnerability creates fertile ground for narcissistic patterns to develop, particularly when combined with the types of childhood experiences we've discussed. The interplay between genetic predisposition and environmental triggers helps explain why narcissism often appears to run in families, even when parenting styles differ significantly.

The specific origins vary greatly from person to person, but the result is the same: a fragile inner self that feels fundamentally flawed, unlovable, or inadequate. This wounded core is so painful, so intolerable, that the developing child constructs elaborate defenses to avoid ever feeling it again.

Think of it like this: Imagine a child with a wound so deep and painful that they build an entire fortress around it, complete with moats, drawbridges, and armed guards. Over time, they forget the fortress was built to protect a wound, and they come to believe that *they are* the impenetrable fortress.

This doesn't excuse the pain they've caused you. Understanding the wounded child within the narcissist doesn't obligate you to endure their adult cruelty. But it does help explain why traditional approaches to relationship issues—honest communication, compromise, vulnerability, empathy—fail so miserably with narcissistic partners. It explains the frustration you feel when you desperately want to apply or share the advice from *relationship experts*, but you know these strategies would never fly in the Cat-and-mouse game.

You've been trying to reach someone who is not there. You've been appealing to someone's capacity for empathy that was dried up long ago. You've been seeking mutuality with someone who doesn't view you worthy of equitable treatment.

The Two Faces of Narcissism: Grandiose and Vulnerable

Not all narcissists look alike. Researchers and clinicians recognize two primary presentations: grandiose and vulnerable narcissism (Pincus et al., 2014).

Grandiose narcissists display the stereotypical traits we associate with narcissism: overt arrogance, entitlement, and superiority. They're often charismatic, socially dominant, and outwardly confident. When threatened, they respond with aggression, contempt, or rage.

Vulnerable narcissists present differently. They may appear shy, insecure, or hypersensitive. They seek sympathy rather than admiration, positioning themselves as misunderstood victims or unrecognized geniuses. When threatened, they respond with hurt, withdrawal, or passive aggression.

Many narcissists oscillate between these states, appearing grandiose in some contexts and vulnerable in others. This shifting presentation adds another layer of confusion for you. One day, they're the confident, charismatic person you fell in love with; the next, they're a wounded victim needing your care and reassurance.

What unites both types is their fundamental self-absorption and lack of empathy. Whether demanding your admiration or your sympathy, the focus remains steadfast on their needs, their feelings, their narrative.

The Masked Void: Understanding the False Self

What makes narcissistic abuse so confusing is the gap between appearance and reality. The person who charmed you in the *Hunt* phase of the game, promised you the world, and seemed to adore you wasn't entirely fake. But, he wasn't entirely real either.

Psychologists call it the "false self"—a carefully constructed persona designed to elicit admiration, hide vulnerability, and maintain the narcissist's fragile self-esteem (Winnicott, 1960). This isn't the same as the ordinary social masks we all wear in different contexts and environments. It's more fundamental, more all-encompassing.

Behind the mask lies what many therapists call "the void"—an emptiness where a stable sense of self would typically reside. Without a solid identity at their core, the narcissist must constantly seek external validation, or "narcissistic supply," to maintain their constructed sense of self and worth.

This explains the insatiable hunger for admiration. The constant need for attention. The extreme reactions to perceived slights. The nagging fear of being alone. They're not just being difficult; at the core, they're fighting for psychological survival.

A Day in the Life of Narcissistic Exhaustion

Consider what a day-in-the-*exhausted*-life of a Cat may look like—battling their unfulfilled, insecure self on one hand, and you, the mouse, on the other.

Morning begins with the Cat awakening to that familiar gnawing emptiness. Before even rising from bed, they check social media, hunting for overnight validation (e.g., likes, comments, any morsel of admiration) to temporarily fill the void. The mirror becomes the first battlefield; they scrutinize every flaw, every sign of aging or imperfection that threatens their carefully manufactured image. "I need to get my teeth whitened." If you're there, you might receive a cleverly critical comment cloaked in concern about your appearance; it's a projection of their own insecurities neatly transferred onto you.

Is your Cat gainfully employed? By mid-morning, the workplace becomes another arena for psychological warfare. Every email, meeting, and interaction is filtered through his fragile ego. A colleague's innocent question becomes a challenge to his authority, or worse, his *manhood.* A boss's constructive feedback registers as a devastating attack. He responds by either dominating conversations with exaggerated accomplishments or withdrawing into sullen resentment. Meanwhile, actual work piles up, creating real-world consequences he'll later blame on colleagues or "home life" with you.

If your Cat is *not* gainfully employed, the busywork required for their 29th business idea continues with all fervency and importance. The Intelligent mouse has the right to remain silent; any slight question, suggestion, idea, or offer to help that he perceives as a threat to his constructed genius will be used against you in a future argument, or immediately dealt with.

Back to the working Cat. Lunchtime offers no respite. Social interactions become performances where they *must* simultaneously be the director and the star. Every conversation must circle back to them, every anecdote shared by others is merely a prompt for their grander story. If he's lunching with you, he might oscillate between love-bombing ("No one understands me at work like you do"), and subtle put-downs ("Did you look in the mirror before you left the house today?") designed to keep you off-balance.

The afternoon brings mounting tension as the day's accumulated narcissistic injuries take their toll. Reality fails, yet again, to conform to their grandiose expectations. They might retreat into fantasy—elaborate daydreams where they're finally recognized as the exceptional being they believe themselves to be. Or, perhaps they'll seek quick relief by spending money they don't have (but you do, and "you" is we), picking fights with random service workers they feel superior to, or sending slick, provocative text messages to potential sources of fresh narcissistic supply.

Evening arrives, and home should be a sanctuary. Instead, it's where the most intense battles are fought.

If you've had a success that day, watch how quickly they diminish it or claim credit for it. "Anybody with common sense could've landed that small account." "I was the one who referred you", as if their referral without your tireless work and follow-through was a guaranteed slam dunk. If you express a need, observe how it's twisted into evidence of your neediness or selfishness. Dinner conversation becomes a minefield; your opinions dismissed, your words constantly interrupted, your emotions manipulated. Perhaps they'll weaponize silence, or withhold affection until you beg for forgiveness for imagined slights.

Multiply this by 10,000 for an unemployed Cat, who will punish you for a win he knows he can't legitimately claim, but wants to. The envy is evidenced by his rejection of intimate advancements with, "I don't make the money you're able to make. I can't afford to hug/touch/kiss you."

As night falls, the Cat grows more desperate. The day's accumulated failures to secure adequate narcissistic supply leave them irritable and dangerous. They might launch into a rage over a minor household issue, creating a crisis that ensures all attention remains fixed on them. Or, they might suddenly become the victim, collapsing at the foot of the bed into tears over how misunderstood they are, how no one—especially you—appreciates their struggles and sacrifices. Your attempts to empathize or comfort repulse them, and you'll hear, "Get away from me. It ain't real. I have to become weak like this before you care?"

Bedtime brings no peace. Another round of silent treatment, this time with nonchalant whistling that signals a lack of concern for your emotional discomfort. If they've failed to extract sufficient validation from you or others, they may lie awake, scrolling through phones or tablets, playing video games for the win that eluded them all day, hunting for one last hit of admiration before his *broken* sleep. Or, perhaps they'll wait until you're right at the cusp of slumber to wake you up with an urgent "We need to talk." It's the same issue from your college dating years that somehow has resurfaced for the 458th time as a fatal issue. "Remember that time when you said/did..." Resolution always ends with demands for your apologies (again), you understanding how much you hurt them, you promising to do better, you soothing his fragile ego so everyone can finally get some sleep before the alarm goes off.

But the Cat doesn't rest well, does he? Late night TV. Questionable late-night texts to women you don't know. He's tormented emotionally, mentally, spiritually, and nothing but tossing and turning as usual. His restless nights signal you to prepare for the morning landmines; "How will I justify my sound sleep, snoring and all, while he tossed and turned all night?"

The morning alarm sounds. Will the new day bring Dr. Jekyll or Mr. Hyde, again? This is where you pray for *any* flavor of Dr. Jekyll; you just need a moment to breathe. This exhausting cycle isn't a conscious strategy for the Cat. It's psychological survival for someone you love but can't save.

Narcissistic Defenses: How They Protect Themselves from Reality

To maintain their grandiose self-image and avoid the pain of their wounded core, narcissists employ sophisticated psychological defenses:

Denial: The refusal to acknowledge reality when it threatens their self-image. "I never said that" (even when you have hard proof they did).

Projection: Attributing their own unacceptable qualities or feelings to others. "You're so selfish" (when they're the ones being selfish).

Splitting: Viewing people and situations in black-and-white terms. You're either perfect and idealized or worthless and devalued; there is no middle ground.

Rationalization: Creating elaborate justifications for their behavior. "I had to lie because you wouldn't understand the truth, and I didn't want to hear your mouth!"

Gaslighting: Manipulating you into questioning your own reality, memory, and perceptions. "You're over-reacting to nothing." or "That never happened."

These defenses are automatic psychological mechanisms that protect the narcissist from intolerable feelings of shame, inadequacy, or vulnerability.

The problem is that while these defenses protect the narcissist, they devastate you. You're left questioning your sanity, doubting your worth, and tiptoeing around your own needs to avoid triggering their rage.

Cat Tactics Decoded: The Narcissist's Manipulation Playbook

In this chapter's exploration of narcissistic psychology, let's decode the specific manipulation tactics that stem directly from the narcissist's personality:

Projection as Weapon: "You're so controlling," says the person monitoring your every move. "You never listen," claims the one who won't let you complete a thought without interruption. Narcissists project their own flaws onto you with such conviction that you begin to wonder if they're right. This isn't just hypocrisy; it's a psychological defense that protects them from acknowledging their own unacceptable qualities by relocating them to you instead.

Selective Memory Manipulation: Narcissists don't just forget inconvenient facts; they actively rewrite history. Promises they made disappear. Abusive incidents never happened. Your accomplishments fade while theirs grow more impressive in the retelling. This isn't mere forgetfulness but an unconscious editing of reality to maintain their self-image and their control over you.

Triangulation Tactics: Introducing third parties into your relationship dynamic serves multiple purposes for the narcissist. They might praise another woman to make you jealous, quote "everyone" who agrees with them against you, or tell conflicting stories to different people to isolate you. This creates a web of confusion where you're constantly off-kilter, competing for position, and unable to trust your social connections.

Intermittent Reinforcement Programming: Perhaps their most powerful tool, narcissists instinctively know how to keep you hooked via unpredictable rewards. Like our trusty slot machine example, they pay out just often enough to keep you playing. The Cat provides affection, approval, or connection just when you're ready to give up. This creates a powerful biochemical addiction more difficult to break than consistent abuse itself.

Mouse Traps: The Psychological Strongholds That Keep You Stuck

Proverbs 22:24-25 ISV tells us, "Don't make friends with a hot-tempered man, and do not associate with someone who is easily angered, or you may learn his ways and find yourself caught in a trap." Your intelligence, compassion, and capacity to love the difficult have been turned into traps. Here are the specific psychological strongholds that keep smart women tied to narcissists:

The Fixer Trap: Your natural empathy recognizes the wounded child beneath the narcissist's defenses. You see their pain, even when they don't. This activates your nurturing instincts and problem-solving abilities. "If I can just help them heal the root of their wounds, the loving person I first met will return permanently." This trap exploits your compassion and depth, keeping you invested in their healing while your own wounds multiply.

The Mirror Trap: After months or years of having the narcissist's negative qualities projected onto you, you begin to see yourself through their distorted lens. "Maybe I am too sensitive. Maybe I do expect too much. Maybe I am the crazy one." This trap uses your capacity for self-reflection against you, turning healthy introspection into destructive self-doubt.

The Potential Trap: Your ability to see possibilities keeps you hooked on who they *could* be rather than who they consistently are. You remember moments of connection, glimpses of vulnerability, flashes of the person you thought you were building a life with. "They're capable of change. I've seen it." This trap exploits your vision and optimism, keeping you invested in a future that exists only in your imagination.

The Comparison Trap: Your intelligence recognizes the complexity of your situation, making you resist "simplistic" solutions. "Other women would just leave, but they don't understand the nuances. Our situation is different." This trap uses your intellectual sophistication against you, keeping you engaged in analyzing a problem that requires action, not further understanding.

These traps are particularly effective against smart, empathetic women. The very qualities that make you exceptional—your emotional intelligence, your commitment, your ability to see beyond the surface—become the chains that bind you to someone incapable of truly loving you back.

Repossess Truth: Steps Toward Seeing Clearly

Understanding the narcissist's psychology is only valuable if it helps you reclaim your own reality. Similar to reclaiming your intelligence, here are some concrete steps toward clarity:

1. **Document reality**: Keep a private journal of incidents, conversations, and patterns. Gaslighting relies on memory manipulation; written records are harder to distort.
2. **Trust your body**: Your physical responses—tension, nausea, fatigue—are often more reliable than your thoughts, which currently can be manipulated. Your body knows you're in danger even when your mind is confused.
3. **Seek external validation**: Find a therapist, support group, or trusted friend who understands narcissistic abuse. You need reality checks from people outside the narcissist's influence.
4. **Study the patterns**: Narcissistic behavior follows predictable cycles. Learning to recognize these patterns can help you respond strategically rather than reactively.

5. **Reclaim your narrative**: The narcissist has been telling you who you are. It's time to remember who you were before their definitions took hold, and who you can become without their limitations.

Psalm 34:18 reminds us that "The Lord is close to the brokenhearted and saves those who are crushed in spirit." Even in your most confused and doubtful moments, truth remains available to you. Your experiences are real. Your pain is valid. Your freedom is available.

The Limits of Understanding: What You Need to Accept

As we conclude this brief exploration of narcissistic psychology, there's a painful truth you must confront: *Understanding the narcissist will never be enough to change them.*

Honey, you can comprehend their wounded core, recognize their defenses, and identify their manipulation tactics with perfect clarity. But this knowledge, while empowering for you, cannot transform them. Why?

1. **Their defenses protect them from insight**: The very psychological mechanisms we've discussed prevent narcissists from achieving the self-awareness necessary for change.
2. **Change requires acknowledging pain**: Meaningful transformation would require them to face the wounded core they've spent a lifetime avoiding.
3. **Their current behavior serves them**: Despite occasional consequences, their manipulative patterns get them what they want most of the time.
4. **You cannot be their healer and their victim at the same time**: The dual role is impossible. Their healing, if it ever comes, must happen far from you and the dynamics that have harmed you both.

This isn't about giving up hope. It's about redirecting it where it belongs: toward your healing, your growth, your future.

For now, hold this truth close: The Cat's behavior reflects their brokenness, not your worth. Their limitations define them, not you. Their inability to love properly reveals nothing about your lovability and everything about their emptiness.

In the next chapter, we'll explore the Cat's selection process and the age-old question, "why me?" With each piece of knowledge, each moment of clarity, you move one step closer to finishing your freedom puzzle.

7

Chapter 7: Why the Cat Hunts

Have you ever wondered why, out of all the women in the world, the Cat chose you? Treats *you* like this?

I remember asking myself this question in the darkest hours of night, when low self-esteem smothered me like a weighted blanket. I kept wondering if there's something fundamentally broken in me that attracted this particular brand of suffering. If you're like me, perhaps you've even blamed yourself for not seeing the red flags in the red carpet sooner.

The truth about why the Cat hunts the mouse is both simpler and more complex than many women realize. And understanding this paradoxical truth is essential to your healing.

In this chapter, we'll examine the predatory nature of narcissistic abuse. We'll uncover why narcissists select particular victims, what they're truly seeking, and most importantly, why being chosen says more about your strengths than your weaknesses. Isn't that wild?

As Proverbs 4:23 reminds us, "Above all else, guard your heart, for everything you do flows from it." To guard your heart effectively, it's important to understand what makes it such a valuable target for the emotional terrorist in the first place.

The Fundamental Drive: Control as Motivation

At the core of every narcissistic relationship lies an insatiable hunger for control. Not the healthy kind of control we all seek over our own lives, but a pathological need to dominate another human being's reality.

For the narcissist, controlling you isn't just a means to an end. It is the end. The ultimate goal. The prize itself.

Why, Kim? Because control creates the illusion of safety for someone whose inner world feels chaotic and threatening. When a narcissist can predict and manipulate your emotions, thoughts, and behaviors, they temporarily soothe their own profound insecurity.

Think about it. When has the Cat's pounce been most dangerous? When you've asserted yourself. When you've challenged their version of reality. When you've set a boundary. When you've threatened their complete dominion over the relationship.

What Control Looks Like

The Cat's control takes many forms:

Emotional control: Dictating what feelings are acceptable for you to express, when, where, and how much. Punishment and consequences appear when you get it wrong.

Psychological control: Gaslighting you until you question your own perceptions. Rewriting history until your memories align with their preferred narrative.

Behavioral control: Monitoring your movements. Isolating you from support systems. Creating rules about everything from how you dress to how you load the dishwasher or open a can of dog food.

Financial control: Restricting your access to money. Creating dependency. Punishing financial independence.

Spiritual control: Twisting faith to justify abuse. Perverting biblical concepts like forgiveness and submission to maintain power.

As a form of psychological survival, the narcissist genuinely believes that if they can't control you completely, they risk annihilation. Their fragile sense of self depends on your total compliance.

In Genesis 3:1, we see how the serpent's first tactic was to make Eve question reality: "Did God really say...?" This ancient conversation captures the essence of narcissistic control and linguistic warfare (Chapter 3). First, make the target doubt what they know to be true. Then, offer an alternative reality where the controller defines what's real, what's valuable, what's permitted.

Hunger Games: Supply My Needs, Please.

"Narcissistic supply" isn't just a psychological term. It's the fuel that keeps the narcissist functioning. Without it, they experience what therapists call "narcissistic collapse"—a state of depression, rage, and emptiness that feels unbearable (Kernberg, 2018).

Think of narcissistic supply as emotional oxygen. The narcissist literally cannot survive without it. And you, the mouse, were selected as a particularly rich source of this essential resource.

What exactly constitutes this supply?

Narcissistic supply looks and feels like:

Admiration—Your genuine appreciation for their talents, knowledge, achievements, or qualities.

Attention—Your focused engagement, whether positive or negative.

Adoration—Your love, devotion, and prioritization of their needs.

Accommodation—Your willingness to adapt, compromise, bend, and make sacrifices.

Acquiescence—Your eventual surrender of will, boundaries, and independent thought.

The narcissist assesses potential targets for their capacity to supply. How much can they extract? How long will it last? How easily can it be harvested?

This explains why narcissists constantly target High-value women. Contrary to popular belief, they don't seek out the weak, insecure, or desperate. What could a mouse like that offer them? How could *she* make him feel better about his insecure, empty self? No, instead they hunt for the strong, the capable, the compassionate, the accomplished. They hunt for the Beautiful, Intelligent, Tenacious, Courageous, High-value (B.I.T.C.H.) woman.

Sis, your strength wasn't a deterrent. It was the attraction.

The biblical story of Samson and Delilah illustrates this dynamic perfectly. Delilah targeted Samson because of his strength. His power was precisely what made possessing him valuable. And like many narcissists, she identified his vulnerabilities—his trust, his love, his blind spots—and exploited them to gain control of his strength. But in the end, there's still hope for the hunted to take back their strength.

The Hunting Toolkit: Lure, Capture, and Keep

A smart predator knows that what it takes to lure prey differs from what it takes to capture prey. And, the tactics used for capture differ from those used to keep the prey. All of the tools in the Cat's bag work together for narcissistic abuse to be effective. Let's take a look at a few of their intricate must-haves; do you recognize any of these tactics?

Value and Boundary Mining: Early conversations seem deeply intimate as they excavate your values, dreams, and worldview. "I've never met anyone who understands me like you do." This isn't a coincidence. They're strategically gathering intelligence on what matters to you so they can present themselves as your *perfect match*. They test your boundaries with small violations, watching how you respond. Do you pop off at the mouth? Shrink yourself to keep the peace? These tests assess how much abuse you'll tolerate later. Responding to your discomfort with phrases like "I was just joking," and "You're overreacting" calibrate their understanding of your resistance threshold.

Vulnerability Scans and Shares: The Cat pays careful attention to what wounds you carry. I reeked of childhood trauma, sexual abuse, and Daddy issues. Past relationship betrayals. Insecurities about your appearance, intelligence, or worth all become their *access points* later. When they say, "You're being too sensitive, just like your daddy always said," they're activating vulnerable trigger points. When told, "You're going to be alone, just like your

Mama!", that was a missed red flag that my vulnerability to abandonment was being used against me. When it comes to what they "reveal" about themselves, they share calculated "intimate" disclosures designed to make you feel special while creating false equivalence. "I've never told anyone this before, but my ex was abusive, too." These seemingly vulnerable moments create artificial intimacy, which make you feel obligated to reciprocate with real vulnerability.

Identity Infiltration and Projection: Emotional terrorists don't just enter your life; they infiltrate your identity. They adopt your interests, mirror your communication style, and align with your values. They don't just present you with a positive version of themselves; they present themselves as *specifically* what you're looking for. And not only you, but the values of your closest friends and family. Longing for someone spiritual? They showcase profound faith and biblical acumen. Valuing intelligence? They display impressive knowledge on subjects where you lack deep understanding. Seeking financial stability? They hint at wealth or potential payoffs. This chameleon-like adaptation is tailored to your particular desires. "Baby, it's like we're the same person!" No, it's like they're wearing your personality as a mask and cloak to gain access to your trust.

Scarcity and Acceleration: They create artificial urgency and exclusivity. "I've never felt this way about anyone." "You're the only one who truly gets me." "We have something special that most people never find." This manufactured scarcity makes you feel seen, chosen, special, and less likely to question red flags. They push for rapid relationship advancement, not from genuine connection but to secure *their* investment before you can properly vet them. "Girl, when you know, you know." "Life is too short, why wait?" "I've never been so sure about anyone in my life." This rush prevents you from noticing inconsistencies or taking the time to seek input from your trusted circle.

These tools are calculated strategies designed to identify High-value targets and secure their compliance. The sophistication of these approaches explains why Intelligent, insightful women still fall prey to being hunted rather than genuinely pursued. Each tactic bypasses rational thought and targets your most human need for connection, understanding, and validation.

The Perfect Prey: Why They Chose YOU

"But, what did I do to deserve this treatment?"

If you've asked yourself this question, you're not alone. The love, patience, sacrifice, and commitment you've shown the Cat doesn't match the energy he's giving back. But think a second...is that the right question? Here's a better one: "What qualities made me so valuable to someone who feeds on others?"

The narcissist didn't choose you for your flaws. He chose you for your virtues. Let's examine some of the specific qualities that make someone like you an ideal target:

Empathy—Your ability to understand others' emotions, to feel and care deeply about their pain, to prioritize their well-being. The narcissist is void of this quality but recognizes it's value. Your empathy means you'll work tirelessly to understand them, make excuses for their behavior, and sacrifice yourself to ease their suffering.

Conscientiousness—Your sense of responsibility, your follow-through, your reliability. While they avoid accountability, they need someone who will pick up the slack, manage the details, and keep life functioning.

Tenacity and Resilience—Your ability to endure hardship, to bounce back from setbacks, to keep trying despite difficulty is a goldmine. This quality ensures you won't give up easily when the abuse begins. You, like me, will keep working to fix the relationship long after others would have left—and you'll wear this truth like a badge of honor.

Success and competence—Your achievements, skills, and capabilities. These qualities provide *status by association* and practical benefits. "My wife/girlfriend" replaces your given name in conversations, confirming their ownership. Your success becomes their success with zero to minimal contribution. Your capabilities become resources they can later exploit for their own pursuits.

Optimism—Your tendency to see the best in others, to believe in potential, to hope for positive change. At the height of the Cat's narcissistic behavior, have you ever thought, "God can do anything but fail!"? "I know God can heal our home." This glass-half-full mentality ensures you'll keep giving the Cat chance after chance, keep believing their empty promises, keep investing in the slim possibility of improvement.

Strong values—Your commitment to concepts like loyalty, honesty, family, faith, and integrity. These values can be weaponized to keep you trapped. "If you leave, you're giving up." "If you were truly forgiving, you'd let this go and move on."

In Psalm 139:14, King David writes, "I praise you because I am fearfully and wonderfully made; your works are wonderful, I know that full well." The qualities that God gave you made you attractive to the narcissist. They are evidence of how intentionally fabulous you truly are.

No one ever tries to dim darkness. The narcissist saw in you what they lack in themselves—light! They recognized your light and sought to possess it, control it, and ultimately, extinguish it.

Cat Tactics Decoded: Predatory Patterns in Narcissistic Abuse

Narcissistic abuse isn't random. It follows predictable patterns. Understanding these patterns helps you recognize that what happened to you was calculated, not accidental.

Much like the general cat-and-mouse game, the hunt typically unfolds in similar phases:

1. **The Stalking Phase**: Before you even noticed them, they were watching. "Who is she?" Assessing. Learning your strengths and vulnerabilities. What do you value? What do you fear? What do you need? This information gathering may seem like getting-to-know-you *casual conversations*, but it's more strategic.
2. **The Pounce (Love Bombing)**: Once they've identified you as suitable prey, they strike with overwhelming, feel-good force. Excessive compliments. Rapid intimacy. Mirroring your values, interests, and dreams. Future-faking about the life you'll build together. This phase creates a powerful biochemical bond that will make later phases harder to escape.
3. **The Capture (Isolation)**: Slowly, they separate you from your herd.

77

Small comments about your friends. Questions about your family's intentions. "They're just jealous of *you* and don't want to see *us* happy." Manufactured emergencies and guilt trips that prevent you from attending social events. Manipulating scenarios where it's you and them against the world.

4. **The Kill (Devaluation)**: Once you're sufficiently isolated and bonded, the true feeding begins. Your strengths, once praised, become targets for criticism. Your boundaries, once respected, become challenges to overcome. Your reality, once shared, becomes subject to constant revision. The emotional terrorists' fangs are sunk deep into your veins, sucking the light and life out of you.

5. **The Consumption (Discard or Recycling)**: When they've extracted maximum supply or you've begun to resist the abuse, they either discard your shell of a life for new prey or temporarily retreat before beginning the cycle again. The discard is rarely clean or final. They often keep you as a backup supply source, returning if and when new targets prove insufficient.

This cycle is instinctual. The Cat hunts the mouse because that's what cats do. Understanding this can help you depersonalize the abuse.

In John 10:10, Jesus says, "The thief comes only to steal and kill and destroy; I have come that they may have life, and have it to the full." The narcissist is a thief, seeking to steal your joy, kill your confidence, and destroy your sense of self.

Mouse Traps: The Psychological Binds That Keep You Confused

Even when you begin to recognize the predatory nature of the relationship, specific psychological traps can keep you from fully accepting that you were targeted:

The Specialness Trap: "But he chose me out of everyone." This trap confuses being targeted with being valued. The lion doesn't select the gazelle out of admiration. The narcissist's focused attention feels like a compliment, but it's actually assessment and acquisition.

The Coincidence Trap: "We had so much in common. It must have been meant to be." This trap ignores the deliberate mirroring that narcissists employ. Those "amazing coincidences" in values, interests, and dreams were manipulated to create false intimacy.

The Perfection Trap: "No relationship is perfect. Everyone has problems." This trap normalizes abuse by equating it with ordinary relationship challenges. Arguments about household chores are normal. Systematic reality distortion and emotional manipulation are not.

The Responsibility Trap: "If I was targeted for my strengths, then I'm responsible for attracting this abuse." This trap confuses understanding with blame. Recognizing why you were selected doesn't make the predator's choices your fault. The gazelle isn't responsible for the lion's hunger.

These traps exploit your intelligence against you. They create logical-seeming frameworks that keep you engaged in analyzing what happened rather than accepting the predatory nature of the relationship and taking action to protect yourself.

The Ultimate Truth: The Hunt Was Never Really About You

As we conclude this exploration of why the Cat hunts the mouse, there's a paradoxical truth to remember: *The narcissist chose you for your exceptional qualities, but their abuse was never about you at all.*

You were selected for your strengths, but the subsequent devaluation, criticism, and cruelty weren't responses to your failures or flaws. Their false accusations revealed their fears. Their criticisms exposed their insecurities. Their rage displayed their fragility.

Understanding this doesn't excuse their behavior. It simply helps you stop internalizing it. Once I stopped internalizing the Cat's behavior, I could stop internalizing a home-grown belief that I was obligated to fix it. His words and actions reflected his reality and core, not mine. Their perception of you was distorted by their own damaged lens.

In Matthew 7:16, Jesus says, "By their fruit you will recognize them." The narcissist's behavior—the fruit of their character—reveals who they truly are. Not their charming words. Not their occasional kindness. Not their promises to change. Their consistent patterns of behavior speak the truth their words disguise.

So, hold *this* truth close: You were hunted not because you were weak, or flawed, but because you were gifted. Not because you deserved abuse, but because you carried a light the narcissist wanted to possess.

In the next chapter, we'll explore how the Cat recruits others to assist in their hunt. Understanding the dynamics of flying monkeys and enablers will help you navigate the social complexities of abuse and recognize why others may not believe your experiences.

Regardless, you were fearfully and wonderfully made long before the Cat entered your life, and you remain so now, despite the wounds inflicted.

You are not defined by being hunted. And your story doesn't end with being caught.

8

Chapter 8: The Supporting Cast—Flying Monkeys and Enablers

"Stop being deceived. Wicked friends lead to evil ends." - 1 Corinthians 15:33 ISV
"No weapon turned against you will succeed. You will silence every voice raised up to accuse you." - Isaiah 54:17 NLT

Newsflash: The Cat doesn't hunt alone.

What fun would all of that stalking, pouncing, capturing, killing, and consuming be in isolation (Chapter 7)?

Oh, they *want* you to think they do. They want you to believe that your relationship exists in a vacuum, that the problems between you two are private matters that should stay behind closed doors. But the truth is far more sinister. The Cat has assembled an entire supporting cast to help him maintain his facade and execute the terror attacks on your emotions with precision and success.

Welcome to the world of *flying monkeys and enablers*, where *your* reality becomes a minority opinion and the truth gets buried under a chorus of voices that tell you you're wrong, you're overreacting, and you're the real problem.

If you've ever wondered why you're getting those awkward looks from family, friends, or strangers, or why no one believes you when you try to explain what's happening behind closed doors, this chapter will provide the answers you've been seeking.

The Flying Monkey Phenomenon

The term "flying monkey" comes from L. Frank Baum's *The Wonderful Wizard of Oz*, where the Wicked Witch sends actual winged jungle monkeys to do her bidding. In the narcissist's world, flying monkeys are the people who carry out the Cat's agenda, often without realizing they're being manipulated themselves.

It all depends. These aren't bad people necessarily. In fact, many flying monkeys are genuinely caring individuals who believe they're helping. They've been fed a carefully crafted narrative about you, the relationship, and the Cat's victimhood. They see themselves as peacemakers, problem-solvers, or loyal friends who love you both. Many times, they have no idea they're participating in emotional and psychological warfare.

Let's face it, sis. The Cat is a master storyteller, and they've been crafting your villain origin story long before you even knew there was a problem. While you were trying to save the relationship or protect *their* image, they were busy painting you as the unstable one, the difficult one, the violent one, the cheating one, the one who "just doesn't understand them."

I'll never forget when I caught wind of the Cat taking *unbiased surveys* from co-workers and friends about our relationship. Not unbiased as *free from all prejudice and favoritism*, but the Cat's decoded definition of "people who don't know the mouse, and thus won't raise any opposition to my lies." Here's an example: "Hey, man. I got a simple question. Nothing really wrong, just a general question. If your woman thought/believed/said/wanted X, how would you handle that?"

Now. Here's the problem: The Cat will try to convince you that he has the capacity to *honestly* and adequately share your feelings, meanings, and intentions with others. Collecting genuine feedback on manipulated issues is a page ripped from the center of the emotional terrorist's playbook, chapter on flying monkeys—"Flying Monkey Assets: How to Build Your Team of Loyalists While Lying in Plain Sight". Survey says? A verbal barrage of "See, Kim! See, you want me to think *I'm* crazy. Any other man would think/feel/do the same thing!"

Sometimes, flying monkeys are not overtly hostile. They come bearing messages of reconciliation, pleas for understanding, and gentle suggestions that maybe you should "try to see things from his perspective." Their sincerity makes the manipulation even more devastating.

The biblical warning about wolves in sheep's clothing applies perfectly here. These people may look like helpers, but they're actually extensions of the Cat's reach into your life. They become the Cat's eyes and ears, reporting back on your emotional state, your plans, your social media posts, or your support system. They become the Cat's voice, delivering messages and points of view, and applying pressure with the Cat's paw without them even being present.

The Smear Campaign: Rewriting Your Story

Before you even realize you're under attack, the Cat has already begun rewriting your story. Not random gossip or casual complaining. It is a systematic campaign to destroy your credibility and isolate you from potential support.

The smear campaign typically begins during the relationship, not after it ends. While you're still trying to make things work, the Cat is already planting seeds of doubt about your mental stability, your character, and your version of events. They share carefully selected "concerns" about the relationship, your behavior, your reactions, and your "inability to make them happy."

They might tell their mother that you're "going through a difficult time" and seem "really unstable lately." Now, decode the tactic, ladies: they must not come off too harsh or antagonistic. Remember, the smear campaign is often cloaked in manufactured concern and support. They might confide in a mutual friend that they're "worried about your mental health" because you've been "acting crazy lately." On the other hand, they might share with *the boys* that you're "really controlling" and "don't understand the daily pressures men are under."

Sometimes the smear campaign is love bomb bait for a possible new supply.

One of my many smear campaign readers was a local actress and model who was going through a tough time finding work, juggling car trouble, etc. The Cat, of course being a "good guy and a good friend", would offer to take her places, accompany her to court, etc. These friendly deeds turned into flirtatious texts after midnight, private inside jokes, and consistent "Good morning" messages. By the time I pushed past the gaslighting of "you're so insecure, you're just jealous that my friends look better than you", the text messages had escalated to, "I'm not getting what I need at home. I need your ear." One strong smear campaign, if executed with precision, can produce a double-win for the emotional terrorist: your image is tarnished, and a new supply becomes empathetic to the Cat's suffering.

Each conversation is designed to accomplish multiple goals. First, it positions the Cat as the long-suffering, patient partner who's trying their best to salvage the relationship and help you through your "issues." Second, it establishes a narrative that explains away any *future* complaints you might make. If you later try to tell someone about the Cat's abusive behavior, they'll already have a framework for deflecting or dismissing your claims as evidence of *your* instability.

The most insidious part of the smear campaign is how it uses your own reactions against you. When you finally reach your breaking point and respond with anger, tears, yelling, or desperation, the Cat points to your reaction as *proof* of everything they've been saying. "See? Why are you in here yelling like a crazy woman? This is exactly what I was talking about. You don't see me yelling, do you?"

And if you're like me, no matter how hard you rocked the "I" in B.I.T.C.H., your *intelligence* repeatedly failed you.

Your authentic emotional responses to abuse become evidence of your instability. Your attempts to defend yourself become proof of *your* aggressive abuse. Your efforts to explain what's really happening become confirmation of your paranoia. The Cat has created a narrative so airtight that any evidence you present to the contrary only seems to support their version of events.

Public Persona vs. Private Reality

One of the most maddening aspects of narcissistic abuse is the stark contrast between who the Cat is in public and who they are behind closed doors. This isn't just putting on a good face for company. This is a carefully maintained double-life designed to make you question your own sanity.

To the public, "he's so cool, helpful, and considerate." The Cat remembers everyone's names, asks about their families, and offers assistance when needed. They're always ready with a joke or an encouraging word, the first to volunteer for community projects, and the last to leave when help is needed.

Consider the public image of a community or business leader, a respected teacher, or in my case, an ordained minister and extraordinary singer with the gift of gab and influence. People genuinely like them. Some even admire them and want to be like them.

This public persona serves multiple purposes. It provides the Cat with the narcissistic supply they crave from a wider audience. It creates a stark contrast that makes your private experiences seem impossible to believe. And, it gives them a reputation to fall back on when you try to share what you've experienced with them.

When you attempt to tell someone about the Cat's abusive behavior, you're not just asking them to believe your word against the Cat's. You're asking them to believe that the person they know as kind, generous, fun-loving, and stable is actually cruel, selfish, and manipulative. The cognitive dissonance introduced in Chapter 2 is so strong that many people simply cannot or refuse to make that leap.

The Cat knows this. They've cultivated their public image specifically to make your private reality seem unbelievable. Who would ever picture me locking myself in the bathroom to get away from a minister with a good word and a powerful prayer? They've invested years in building relationships, roles, and establishing credibility so that when the time comes - and it will - their word will carry more weight than yours.

This is why you might find yourself staying silent about the abuse for so long. You're not crazy. You know that if you speak up, you'll be the one who looks "off". You'll be the one disrupting the peace. You'll be the one causing problems for someone everyone else sees as wonderful. And when you count up these costs, it's often cheaper to keep the Cat and the peace.

The isolation this creates for you is profound. It becomes a living mouse trap with no conceivable exit. Depending on your personality, you know if people had to choose between you and the "life of the party," you and "the business leader with all the connections", you didn't stand a chance. And the Cat knows it. I remember having no clever comeback for the words, "People like me better than you. They like you because of me. You're a hard nut to crack." You begin to feel like you're living in an alternate reality where up is down and black is white. You start to question not just your perceptions of the Cat, but your own worth and ability to perceive reality accurately at all.

The Psychology of Enablers

Now, enablers are different from flying monkeys. While flying monkeys are often unwitting participants in the Cat's manipulation, enablers have *some* awareness of the Cat's problematic behavior. They just choose to excuse, minimize, or ignore it. They're not necessarily malicious, but their need to maintain peace, avoid conflict, or preserve their own relationship with the Cat takes precedence over your experience and well-being.

Enablers often have their own history with the Cat that makes them reluctant to challenge the status quo. They might be family members who've learned that confronting the Cat leads to explosive consequences. They might be friends who've seen the Cat's vindictive side and don't want to become the next target. They might be colleagues who depend on the Cat professionally and can't afford to rock the boat.

The enabler's mindset is often rooted in conflict avoidance and self-preservation. They've learned that it's easier to pressure you, the mouse, to "be the bigger person" than to hold the Cat accountable for their behavior. They've discovered that encouraging you to "just let it go" requires less courage than standing up to the Cat's manipulation.

Enablers often use spiritual or moral language to justify their position. They might tell you that forgiveness is divine, that we all make mistakes, that holding grudges is unhealthy, or that family loyalty requires overlooking flaws. They present their enabling as wisdom, their avoidance as peace-making, and their cowardice as virtue.

What enablers don't understand is that their refusal to acknowledge reality doesn't create peace. It creates an environment where abuse flourishes unchecked. Their silence isn't neutral. It's complicity. Their inaction isn't wisdom. It's abandonment.

The most painful enablers, sis, are going to be the people closest to you. Parents who believe the Cat is a "great guy" for picking up their medicine. Siblings who prioritize some form of access or perks over your protection. Friends who value their relationship with the Cat more than your well-being. The Cat's closest friends who err on the side of loyalty when the truth hurts. These betrayals cut deep because they come from people you trusted to value your emotional health over excuses.

Cat Tactics Decoded

Preemptive Strikes: Emotional terrorists operate on the offense only! The Cat shares their version of events before you have a chance to speak. By the time you try to explain what really happened, everyone has already heard the Cat's narrative and formed their opinions. Your truth becomes a "different perspective" on an already established story. How does this happen?

The Silver Bullets of "Not Yet"

The reason the Cat strikes first is simple: in their mind, you've already struck—or you're about to. They've planted a mental bomb, convinced themselves of your betrayal, and now their preemptive attacks feel like self-defense. These shots aren't reactions to your actions; they're reactions to imagined offenses. Remember, the psychological and emotional warfare you're experiencing is real—but it's unfolding inside the Cat's mind. You're just living the projection.

To illustrate the concept of the Cat's "not yet," consider this real-life scenario. The Cat and I invited two long-time friends over for dinner, intending to discuss some relationship challenges in a supportive setting. After catching up and sharing a few laughs over a gourmet meal he prepared, the tone shifted.

"So, what's going on with you two?" one friend asked.

The Cat responded by launching into actions, intentions, and betrayals he claimed I had committed—none of which had occurred. The false accusations were delivered confidently, calmly, and without warning.

Later, when I questioned the false accusations, the Cat replied, "*Well. You haven't done it yet, but you have the capacity to.*"

Pay close attention. This wasn't a misunderstanding. It was strategy. If the Cat can imagine harm, label it real, and persuade others that it's truth, he could justify his victimhood and *pre-punish* the mouse in advance. That's the logic of emotional terrorism: create a threat where none exists, then control through fear of the hypothetical. In the Cat's alternate universe, "not yet" is enough for your guilty verdict.

Concern Trolls: Flying monkeys approach you with apparent concern for your well-being, but their real agenda is to troll and gather information for the Cat, or pressure you to see things from the Cat's lens. They'll ask probing questions about your mental state, your plans, your coping mechanisms, then report back to the Cat. Know the difference between concern and monitoring, the ones always "checking in, you were on my heart."

Character Witnesses: The Cat surrounds themselves with people who can vouch for their character. When you make accusations, these witnesses step forward to testify about the Cat's kindness, generosity, and stability. Your claims seem impossible in light of all this "evidence" to the contrary.

Proxy Punishment: When the Cat can't attack you directly, they'll use flying monkeys to deliver consequences. This includes your own family members who "love" the Cat—even your own children. It is not beneath an emotional terrorist to manipulate your children against the truth in favor of their narratives. The familiar words and phrases only the Cat would know, but spoken by the flying monkey, is all the proof you need. You might find yourself excluded from social events, criticized by mutual friends, or subjected to passive-aggressive comments from people who've been fed negative information about you.

Mouse Traps

The Explanation Trap: You believe that if you could just explain what really happened, people would understand and support you. But the Cat has already shaped the narrative, and your explanations often sound defensive or paranoid to people who've been primed to see you as unstable.

The Proof Trap: You think that if you could just provide enough evidence, people would believe you. But emotional abuse rarely leaves visible scars, and the Cat's public persona provides counter-evidence that seems more credible than your private experiences. Plus, any masterful gaslighter can explain away even the hardest receipts.

The Loyalty Trap: You expect the same loyalty from others that you would give them. You can't understand why people who claim to care about you would choose to believe the Cat's lies over the truth. This expectation sets you up for repeated disappointment and betrayal. You don't have to excuse their free will, but it must be accepted.

The Isolation Acceptance: You gradually withdraw from social situations to avoid the pain of not being believed or supported. This isolation plays right into the Cat's hands, removing potential witnesses to their behavior and sources of support for you.

Breaking Free from the Supporting Cast

Understanding the dynamics of flying monkeys and enablers is crucial for your healing journey, but it's also one of the most painful aspects of recovery. Realizing that the people you trust have been manipulated against you, or worse, have chosen to enable your abuse, can feel like a second betrayal.

Here's what you need to understand: you cannot control other people's choices, but you can control your response to them. You cannot force people to see the truth, but you can stop trying to convince them. You cannot make enablers choose courage over comfort, but you can choose to surround yourself with people who don't require you to minimize your pain for their peace of mind.

The hard truth is that some relationships won't survive your awakening—and that's okay. Some people are so invested in the Cat's narrative, or so committed to avoiding conflict, that they'll choose the lie over the truth. This isn't a reflection of your worth or the validity of your experiences. It's a reflection of their character and their priorities.

Scripture reminds us that "a friend loves at all times, and a brother is born for a time of adversity" (Proverbs 17:17). The people who abandon you during your darkest hour were never truly your forever-friends to begin with. The people who require you to stay silent about your abuse to maintain their comfort were never truly your allies.

Your job isn't to convince everyone of your truth. Your job is to honor *the* truth and surround yourself with people who honor it, too. Your job isn't to make everyone comfortable with your healing. Your job is to heal, regardless of who finds that process inconvenient.

The Cat's supporting cast only has power if you continue to seek their approval and validation. When you stop trying to convince them, when you stop explaining yourself to people who've already decided not to believe you, when you stop accepting crumbs of conditional support from people who should be offering you full meals of unconditional love, their influence over your life begins to diminish.

Do you think we've cracked the mask of the Cat, and you can see clearly now what lies beneath? Well, think again. In the next chapter, we'll take a deeper dive into the mastermind puppeteer behind all forms of emotional terrorism.

For now, remember this: the people who matter don't need convincing, and the people who need convincing don't matter. The truth doesn't require a majority vote to be valid.

It simply is.

9

Chapter 9: The Grand Puppet Master—Unmasking the Spirit Behind Emotional Terrorists

"Be clear-minded and alert. Your opponent, the Devil, is prowling around like a roaring lion, looking for someone to devour." - 1 Peter 5:8 ISV

Sis, there's something you need to understand about the Cat in your life. Something that will fundamentally shift how you see them and this game you've been playing.

Yes, we've spent almost half this book decoding the Cat's tactics and strategies. But, the manipulation, the lies, the cruelty, the calculated destruction of your peace and sanity isn't just human behavior gone wrong. It's spiritual warfare being waged against your soul.

Behind every narcissist stands a puppet master pulling the strings. The Cat may think they're in control, may believe their own grandiose narrative about their superiority and entitlement, but they're actually being used by a force far more cunning than their wounded ego. They're not just broken people acting badly. They're puppets, assets being used by the enemy of your soul.

This chapter isn't about removing personal responsibility from abusive behavior. It's about recognizing that some patterns of destruction are too systematic, too calculated, and too spiritually devastating to be merely emotional. When you're dealing with someone whose very presence seems to drain the life from your spirit, whose words feel like poison in your bloodstream, whose influence leaves you questioning your own sanity and worth, you're not just dealing with flesh and blood. You're dealing with something far darker.

The Ancient Adversary

Scripture tells us that our struggle is not against flesh and blood, but against spiritual forces of evil in the heavenly realms (Ephesians 6:12). The Cat may be the *face* of anger, the lying voice you hear, the unfulfilled hands that hurt you. The Cat stalked you as prey, coveted your light, bombarded you with sweet nothings, but they're not your real enemy. They're a weapon being wielded by the one Jesus called "the father of lies"—the devil, the adversary, Lucifer, Satan (John 8:44).

Satan's strategies haven't changed since the Garden of Eden. He comes to steal, kill, and destroy (John 10:10). He steals your peace, kills your joy, and destroys your sense of self-worth. The cunning adversary can take a single word, like "you won't *surely* die" (Genesis 3:4), and twist your entire belief system of what is true and real. This ain't the making of "The Exorcist". The devil doesn't need to possess someone completely, make them foam at the mouth, or contort their body to use them to destroy the spirit of another person. No, he simply needs to find someone whose unhealed trauma wounds, pride, disobedience, discontentment, and selfishness make them susceptible to his influence.

The narcissist becomes the perfect asset because the depth of their core wounds create an insatiable hunger that can never be filled by human means. Their desperate need for validation, their terror of abandonment, their rage at greatness evading them makes them easy targets for spiritual manipulation. The enemy whispers lies that feel like a soothing truth to their broken souls: "You deserve better. You're special. Everyone else is the problem. You have the right to take whatever you want. You deserve to be happy, to smile."

What makes this spiritual attack so insidious is that the Cat genuinely believes these thoughts are their own. They don't recognize the evil influence shaping their perceptions and driving their behavior. They lack the keys to decode the devil's signature on their terroristic schemes. They think their cruelty is justified, their manipulation is necessary, their destruction of others is somehow righteous. They've become convinced that their victims deserve whatever treatment they receive.

This is why reasoning with a narcissist feels like talking to a brick wall. This is why hard evidence rolls off them like water off a duck's back. This is why they can look you in the eye and lie without flinching. This is why the relationship feels like you're sleeping with an enemy. You're not just dealing with human stubbornness or psychological defense mechanisms. You're dealing with a spiritual blindness that has been deliberately cultivated by the enemy of truth.

The Leviathan Spirit: Pride's Perfect Vessel

In the book of Job, God describes a creature called Leviathan, a sea monster of terrifying power and impenetrable defenses. While scholars debate whether this was a literal creature or a symbolic representation, the spiritual characteristics of Leviathan provide a perfect picture of the force operating through narcissistic abuse.

Job 41:15-17 describes Leviathan's scales: "his back has rows of shields tightly sealed together; each is so close to the next that no air can pass between. They are joined fast to one another; they cling together and cannot be parted." This is the narcissist's relationship with truth. Their defenses are so tightly sealed with pride that the air of Truth cannot penetrate. Real, sacrificial love cannot reach them. Reality cannot touch them.

The Leviathan spirit operates through pride, the very sin that caused Satan's fall from heaven. Isaiah 14:13-14 records the enemy's prideful declaration: "I will ascend to the heavens; I will raise my throne above the stars of God... *I will make myself like the Most High.*" Sound familiar? This is the same spirit that drives narcissistic grandiosity, the Cat's belief that they are above normal human rules, relationships, and responsibilities.

Take note: this type of jihad (or struggle) exposes feelings of inadequacy on one hand, and the identification of true greatness on the other. Let me explain. Before greatness can be coveted, it must first be recognized. Lucifer knew full well that the eminence he craved was far *above* his pay grade. Just as Lucifer targeted the stature and majesty of the Most High God, the narcissist targets your light, your compassion, and all the endearing qualities that God poured into you to make you you.

King of Pride

Leviathan is described as the king over all the children of pride (Job 41:34). It's no coincidence that pride is the defining characteristic of people with strong narcissistic tendencies. The narcissist's inflated sense of self-importance, their belief in their own superiority, their expectation of special treatment, their lack of empathy for others—these are all spiritual manifestations of a prideful spirit that has found a willing host.

The *twisting* nature of Leviathan is particularly relevant to understanding narcissistic behavior. This spirit takes truth and twists it just enough to deform it and make it unrecognizable. It takes your words and twists them into weapons against you.

Have you ever said one thing, only for the Cat to hear the complete opposite? I have. It's like Leviathan coiled up into filters and attached itself to their two ears. Your words are hijacked, twisted, and given random, unbelievably wrong meaning.

One time in particular occurred in the final week of our thirty-two-year relationship. My son and I were both down with COVID, and to his credit, the Cat stepped up. He cooked, cleaned, and made sure we were okay. As he prepared for a well-deserved break to celebrate New Year's Eve with his friends, I texted, "Have a great time with the fellas. I love you. I appreciate all the care you've given us. You're doing a great job, one many couldn't or wouldn't do. Thx."

Instead of receiving the text with gratitude, the night progressed with a manufactured argument: "You don't even like my friends. I can't hang out with the fellas without your control. I've waited on y'all hand and foot and deserve some time to have fun, I deserve to smile!" A heartfelt message was twisted into a false accusation of hate and control. At the time, his response seemed so irrational. Nine months later during the divorce, it made sense— "New Year's boys night" had actually been spent with the new supply he'd ultimately marry. Plot twist.

This is why conversations with narcissists feel so disorienting and circular. You start discussing one thing and somehow end up defending yourself against false accusations you never saw coming. Try to address their behavior and you'll find yourself apologizing for your reaction to their actions. You attempt to set a boundary and discover you're now the one being accused of being controlling and selfish. The twisting is so subtle, so skillful, yet ever so consistent.

The Scales of Deception

The impenetrable scales of Leviathan represent more than just stubbornness or closed-mindedness. They represent a supernatural resistance to truth that goes beyond normal human psychology. When you try to reason with someone under this influence, when you present evidence of their harmful behavior, when you appeal to their conscience or their "love" for you, you're not just hitting psychological defenses. You're hitting spiritual armor that has been specifically forged to repel truth. And you're feeling extremely exhausted, annoyed, and frustrated because all the loving, pleasing, giving, and pleading should have worked by now—and your Tenacious self won't stop trying.

So the massacre of your self-esteem and dignity continues. The narcissist can witness the destruction they cause and feel no remorse. This is why they can see your tears and feel no compassion. They can hear your pain and respond with more cruelty. The scales of pride have made them impervious to the very emotions that make us human. Empathy cannot penetrate them. Guilt cannot reach them. People-pleasing cannot soften them.

The scales also represent the narcissist's ability to compartmentalize their behavior. They can be cruel to you in private and charming to others in public without experiencing one sleepless night. They can lie to your face and believe their own lies. They can use every weapon of mass destruction against you and still see themselves as the victim. Each scale represents a separate reality they've created to protect themselves from the truth of who Leviathan has manipulated them to be.

And when you're cut off from the truth like that, it's only a matter of time before you surrender and start aligning with a lie. Narcissists don't just hide behind the armor; they partner with it. They weaponize confusion. They fake misunderstanding. They act oblivious, not because they are, but because their Oscar-worthy performance buys them more time and more power.

It took decades, but I eventually recognized the tactic. Arguments that felt like war, complete with shouting, false accusations, and threats to leave, would only stop once I collapsed in tears. As long as I stood my ground and demanded to be heard, the Cat escalated. But once I broke, once the tears started flowing and the white flag waved, the battle would suddenly end. He'd soften, embrace me, and say, "We don't need to fight like this, bay. We get angry and say things we don't mean. I don't like to see you like this." You're so depleted mentally and emotionally, even a fake cease-fire and peace agreement that stops the bullets from flying is like water to your parched soul.

It wasn't real remorse and Godly sorrow. It was strategy. The Cat learned how to manipulate the many uses of the scales—to cloak offense in confusion, to make clarity feel like confrontation, and to wear down resistance until surrender looked like peace.

Understanding this spiritual dimension doesn't excuse their behavior, but it does explain why traditional approaches to relationship problems don't work with narcissistic abuse. You can't love or empathize someone out of spiritual bondage. You can't reason with someone whose mind has been sealed against truth. You can't fix someone whose very identity has been built on a foundation of lies whispered by the father of lies himself. Only God can.

The Mouse's Impossible Battle

Here's the truth that might be hard to hear but will ultimately set you free: you alone cannot defeat Leviathan.

It's not you against Moby Dick, sis. You may be a loving woman who cares deeply for the Cat, but you cannot break through those scales with your beauty, intellect, tenacity, courage, or your High-value character. BITCH-ness won't work. You cannot force freedom on someone who refuses to acknowledge their need for deliverance. You cannot win a spiritual battle using human weapons (2 Corinthians 10:4).

This isn't evidence of your inadequacy or lack of faith. This isn't an indictment on the effectiveness of your prayers, or a sign that God didn't hear your cries on behalf of the Cat. This is simply the reality of spiritual warfare—deliverance requires the Cat's participation and surrender.

The mouse's greatest mistake is believing that this is a battle she can win through her own efforts. You try harder, love more, give everything you have, thinking that surely your sacrifice will break through the Cat's defenses. You don't realize that, at the end of the day, even your feminine weapons are like bringing a pink water gun to a nuclear war.

This realization can be devastating at first, and takes some women a long time to fully grasp. It means that all your efforts to save the relationship, all your attempts to reach their heart, all your sacrifices to prove your love have been futile from a human perspective. But it can also be incredibly liberating. It means you're not responsible for fixing something that only God can heal.

The enemy wants you to believe that if you just try harder, love better, or give more, you can break through to the person you fell in love with. This is a lie designed to keep you trapped in an impossible battle, exhausting yourself against an enemy you were never meant to fight.

God's Sovereignty Over Leviathan

While you cannot defeat Leviathan, God can.

Job 41:1 begins with God asking, "Can you pull in Leviathan with a fishhook or tie down its tongue with a rope?" The implied answer is no—we cannot. But the very fact that God is asking the question implies that He can do what we can't.

Psalm 74:14 declares that God "crushed the heads of Leviathan and gave it as food to the creatures of the desert." Isaiah 27:1 prophesies that "the Lord will punish with his fierce, great and powerful sword—Leviathan the gliding serpent, Leviathan the coiling serpent; he will slay the monster of the sea."

This doesn't mean God will automatically heal every narcissist or that every abusive person will experience a miraculous transformation. Free will remains a factor, and some people choose to remain in spiritual bondage rather than submit to God's instruction and healing. But it does mean that the battle belongs to the Lord, not to you.

Your role isn't to defeat the enemy operating through the Cat. If you're a woman of faith, your role is to recognize the spiritual nature of the battle and respond accordingly. This means putting on the full armor of God (Ephesians 6:11-18). This means praying for your enemy while protecting yourself from their attacks. This means trusting God's justice while refusing to enable their destructive behavior.

Most importantly, it means understanding that your worth, your identity, and your future don't depend on winning this battle. God's love for you isn't contingent on your ability to save someone who doesn't want to be saved. The Cat's deliverance is not *your* test to pass. Your value isn't determined by your success in penetrating spiritual shields of pride designed to repel truth.

Cat Tactics Decoded

The Spiritual Deep: The Leviathan spirit operating through the Cat often mimics spiritual language and concepts to maintain control. They might quote scripture to justify their behavior, claim divine calling for their actions, or present themselves as more spiritually mature than you. In my case, I was dealing with an ordained minister; repeated pressure to "Increase my faith", "elevate my walk", and "match his level of spiritual maturity" kept me on my toes and under his magnifying glass. This spiritual manipulation is particularly devastating because it weaponizes your faith and the speed of your spiritual growth against you.

The False Repentance: When confronted with their behavior, the Cat may offer what appears to be genuine repentance, complete with tears, promises, and spiritual language. However, this repentance lacks the fruit of genuine change. You will hear every remorseful clause in the book, which, from a pure heart, would shift the trajectory of the relationship. Counterfeit apologies are a manipulation tactic designed to reset the cycle of abuse, not break it. Godly sorrow leads to true repentance, while manipulated remorse simply adds more time to the game clock.

The Victim Reversal: The Leviathan spirit is masterful at making the Cat appear to be the victim of spiritual attack when you try to set boundaries or expose their behavior. They position your resistance to their abuse as perse-cution, your boundaries as spiritual warfare against them, and your healing as rebellion against God's plan for forgiveness and reconciliation. Exposure becomes revenge, and your experiences become agents of defamation—and many Cats, like mine, are not afraid to sue you and take their show on the road to the nearest courthouse stage. Spoiler alert: their false indictments won't stand against you in the Courts of Heaven.

Mouse Traps

The Savior Complex: You believe that your love, prayers, and spiritual warfare can deliver the Cat from their bondage. While prayer is powerful and God can do miracles, you cannot force someone's deliverance or make yourself responsible for their spiritual condition. This trap keeps you engaged in a battle not meant for you to fight alone.

The Spiritual Hall Pass: You use spiritual concepts like forgiveness, turning the other cheek, and loving your enemies to avoid taking practical steps to protect yourself. Have you ever considered that God gave us only two cheeks? Have you turned your cheeks to the point of whiplash, yet? Were you given your own personal reservoir of unlimited grace and mercy, so the Cat can keep hurting you, lying to you, cheating on you, and dishonoring you? True spiritual maturity includes wisdom to know when to engage and when to withdraw, when to fight and when to flee. To everything, there's a season and purpose.

The Guilt Trap: You feel guilty for recognizing the spiritual aspects of the abuse because it seems unloving or judgmental. And let's be honest, this guilt is often created by the *guilt trips* the Cat projects on you. "You think you're so perfect.. you're so holier than thou. I guess you never make a mistake!" Jesus himself called out spiritual darkness when he encountered it. Discernment isn't condemnation; it's true identification.

The Responsibility Trap: You believe that if the Cat's behavior is spiritually influenced, they're not responsible for their choices. "If Leviathan is that powerful, how can the Cat resist?" Influence is not mind-control; it always leaves room to "choose ye this day". Spiritual influence doesn't remove personal responsibility. People choose whether to resist or yield to spiritual pressure, and they remain accountable for their actions regardless of the source of their temptation.

Walking in Spiritual Authority

Understanding the spiritual dimension of narcissistic abuse changes every-thing about how you respond to it. You stop trying to win arguments and start praying for protection. You stop trying to prove your point and start seeking God's wisdom. You stop trying to change the Cat and start asking God to *change you*—not into someone who tolerates abuse, but into someone who walks in spiritual authority and divine wisdom toward freedom.

This doesn't mean becoming passive or fatalistic. It means recognizing that your "weapons are not carnal but mighty through God for pulling down strongholds." (2 Corinthians 10:4) Your weapons are prayer, truth, righteousness, worship, faith, and the Word of God. Your strategy isn't manipulation, revenge, or control but a complete surrender to God's will and trust in His protection.

When you understand that you're dealing with spiritual forces, you stop taking the Cat's behavior personally. You recognize that their cruelty isn't really about you—it's about the enemy's hatred for everything God loves. You're not being attacked because you're worthless; you're being attacked because God loved you so much and you were worth dying for. Jesus died so you can have a life of abundance, not abuse. I humbly offer you an opportunity to accept Jesus Christ as Lord and Savior, and partner with his unfailing love and power to heal and free you from emotional terrorism, narcissistic abuse. Visit the appendix to learn more.

In the next section, all eyes on you! "How can I heal, break free, find myself again?" Let's do one better and help you discover a healed and whole you you've never imagined. Recovery and healing are personal, not linear. Let's see how we can create a recovery plan that's all your own.

For now, remember: you were not created to be anyone's victim. And, you were also not created to be anyone's savior, either. That role belongs to Jesus alone.

"The Lord will fight for you; you need only to be still." – Exodus 14:14

III

SECTION III: HEALING THE WOUNDED MOUSE

10

Chapter 10: Breaking the Trauma Bond

"It is for freedom that Christ has set us free. Stand firm, then, and do not let yourselves be burdened again by a yoke of slavery." - Galatians 5:1

"I should hate him for what he did!"

What they did to you was wrong, cruel, and unnecessary. You know they've proven to be toxic, manipulative, and dangerous to your well-being. Your rational mind understands all of this perfectly.

So. Why do you still miss him? Why do you still love him? Why do you find yourself checking their social media, driving by their house, or hoping they'll call? Why does the thought of never seeing them again feel like death, even though being with them felt like dying slowly?

The answer isn't that you're weak, stupid, or a sucker for pain. The answer is that you're experiencing something called a *trauma bond* - a powerful psychological and biochemical attachment that forms between an abuser and their victim. It's not love, though it feels like love. It's not weakness, though it makes you feel weak. It's a survival mechanism that your emotions created to help you cope with an impossible situation.

Understanding trauma bonds supports your healing because it's hard to break free from something you don't understand. You can't win the war if you bring the wrong weapons to the battles. This chapter will help you understand exactly what happened to your brain and body during the abuse, why you feel so attached to someone who hurt you, and most importantly, how to break free from this invisible chain that's keeping you trapped.

Breaking a trauma bond is like breaking any other addiction, which is why I couldn't do it on my own—I needed God's very present help. As a byproduct of Leviathan, a trauma bond is just as strong as the scales covering Leviathan's body, where not even air can penetrate the seams. Breaking a trauma bond requires accepting that withdrawals are part of the process. There's a need to develop strategies to manage the cravings that will inevitably come. It's not easy, but it's absolutely possible, and it's essential for your freedom.

Your Body: The Secret Score Keeper

Sis, did you know? In the cat-and-mouse game, your body kept the score.

Every cruel word, every moment of terror, every betrayal, every instance of gaslighting that made you question your own reality has been recorded not just in your memory, but in your nervous system, your muscles, your very cells. The trauma you experienced didn't just hurt your feelings or damage your self-esteem. It was "bonded" to you because it literally rewired your brain and reprogrammed your body's responses to the world around you.

This isn't your fault, and it doesn't mean you're broken beyond repair. It means you're human. God designed your brain and body to do exactly what they did: adapt to survive in dangerous environments. The problem is that these adaptations, which served you well during the abuse, will now cause you problems in your daily life as you pursue freedom and recovery.

The hyper-vigilance that helped you anticipate the Cat's moods might now make it impossible for you to relax in safe situations. The denial that protected you from overwhelming pain might now disconnect you from real joy and happiness. The people-pleasing that kept you safe might now prevent you from setting healthy boundaries.

But here's the good news: the same neuroplasticity (ability of the brain to change and adapt) that allowed your brain to cope with trauma can also help it heal from trauma. Your nervous system can learn new patterns. Your body can remember what safety feels like. Your emotional circuitry can be rewired for connection instead of protection, for joy instead of just survival.

The Science of Trauma Bonding

Trauma bonding isn't a character flaw or a sign of weakness. It's a documented psychological phenomenon that occurs when someone alternates between abuse and affection, creating a powerful biochemical addiction in their victim.

The Biochemical Addiction

During the "good" times of the cat-and-mouse game—when they are loving, attentive, and seemingly perfect—your brain released powerful chemicals including dopamine, oxytocin, and endorphins. These are the same chemicals released during drug use, which is why the highs felt so incredibly high.

Dopamine is the addictive "reward" chemical that makes you want to repeat behaviors that feel good. Oxytocin is the "bonding" hormone that creates attachment and trust. Endorphins are natural painkillers that create feelings of euphoria and well-being.

During the abuse—when they were cruel, cold, or violent—these chemicals were suddenly withdrawn, creating a biochemical crash that felt devastating. Your brain, desperate to feel good again, began craving the return of those chemicals. So, when your abuser inevitably returned with apologies, affection, and kindness (love-bombing), the relief was so intense that it created an even stronger biochemical reward than if they had been kind consistently.

And let's not neglect to highlight the role that sex plays in further cementing the trauma bond. My girls and I have a running inside joke: "You'd be hard-pressed to find a narcissist with bad head." Lol. What does this mean? Exactly what I said—most narcissists are highly attentive, talented, and skilled in the bedroom. It's not just because many are "humping for housing", giving Beautiful, Intelligent, Tenacious, Courageous, High-value women a reason to let them move in with them, support them while they're in between jobs, and use their resources. No, the Cat knows that with the right sexual experience, and the right mouse, intelligence, self-esteem, and high-values can be traded for a false sense of love, connection, and intimacy. It is no coincidence that the trifecta of pleasure biochemicals—dopamine, oxytocin, and endorphins—are also released during sexual intimacy, especially through orgasms.

This cycle of chemical highs and lows literally rewired your brain to become addicted to your abuser. Your brain (and body) learned that they were your source of both pain and pleasure, creating a powerful dependency that had nothing to do with love and everything to do with survival and idolatry.

The Intermittent Reinforcement Schedule

Psychologists have long known that intermittent reinforcement— *unpredictable* rewards mixed with punishment—creates the strongest behavioral conditioning possible. In Chapter 1, we talked about this principle and why it makes gambling so addictive. You never know when the next "win" is coming from them, so you keep playing harder, hoping this time will be different.

The Cat, whether consciously or unconsciously, put you on an intermittent reinforcement schedule. Sometimes they were wonderful, sometimes they were terrible, but you never knew which version you were going to get. This unpredictability kept you constantly on your toes, always hoping for the good times and always trying to avoid triggering the bad times.

The unpredictable nature of their affection also made it more valuable, not less. If someone is always kind to you, you tend to take their kindness for granted. But if someone is usually cruel and occasionally kind, their rare moments of kindness feel like precious gifts that you'll do anything to earn again.

The Stockholm Syndrome Effect

Stockholm Syndrome occurs when hostages develop positive, empathetic feelings toward their captors as a survival mechanism. In abusive relation-ships, a similar dynamic occurs. Your brain, recognizing that you're in danger but unable to escape, begins to identify with your abuser as a way to increase your chances of survival.

You start to see the world through their eyes, adopt their perspective, and even defend them to others. This isn't stupidity or weakness; it's your brain's attempt to create safety in an unsafe situation. If you can become valuable to your abuser, if you can anticipate their needs and avoid triggering their anger, maybe they will change and you can survive.

This psychological adaptation makes it incredibly difficult to see the relationship clearly while you're in it. Your brain's intelligence is literally working against your best interests in an attempt to keep you alive.

Recognizing the Signs of Trauma Bonding

Trauma bonding creates specific patterns of thinking, feeling, and behaving that can be difficult to recognize when they're ongoing . Understanding these signs helps you realize that what you're experiencing is a trauma response, not true love.

Emotional Signs:

- You feel addicted to them despite knowing they're bad for you
- You experience intense highs and lows in the relationship
- You feel like you can't live without them, even though living with them is painful
- You make excuses for their behavior to yourself and others
- You feel responsible for their emotions and behavior
- You experience intense anxiety when they withdraw or threaten to leave
- You feel relief and euphoria when they return after being cruel
- You find yourself constantly obsessing about how to please them, make them happy, or keep them calm

Behavioral Signs:

- You keep returning to them despite promising yourself you wouldn't
- You isolate yourself from friends and family who express concern
- You change your behavior, appearance, or beliefs to please them

- You walk on eggshells to avoid triggering their anger
- You give up your own needs, goals, and interests for the relationship
- You find yourself defending them to people who care about you
- You make excuses for staying in the relationship
- You feel like you need their approval to feel good about yourself

Physical Signs:

- You experience withdrawal symptoms when separated from them (anxiety, depression, physical pain)
- You feel physically ill when the relationship is in crisis
- You experience intense physical relief when they show you affection
- You have trouble sleeping, eating, or concentrating when they're upset with you
- You feel physically addicted to their touch, presence, or attention

Understanding Withdrawal Symptoms

When you decide to break a trauma bond, you will most likely experience intense withdrawal symptoms that are remarkably similar to drug withdrawal. This is because you are literally withdrawing from the biochemical addiction your brain formed to your abuser.

Common Withdrawal Symptoms:

- Intense cravings to contact them or see them
- Physical pain, especially in your chest or stomach
- Anxiety and panic attacks
- Depression and hopelessness
- Insomnia and nightmares
- Loss of appetite or compulsive eating and spending
- Difficulty concentrating or making decisions
- Feeling like you're going crazy or losing your mind

- Obsessive thoughts about them and the relationship
- Physical trembling or shaking

Example Withdrawal Timeline:

Days 1-7: Acute withdrawal with intense physical and emotional symptoms. You may feel like you're dying, can't breathe, or going crazy. This is the most dangerous time for relapse.

Weeks 2-4: Symptoms begin to lessen but are still significant. You may have good days followed by terrible days. Cravings come in waves.

Months 2-6: Gradual improvement with occasional setbacks. You start to have more good days than bad days, but triggers can still cause intense cravings.

Months 6-12: Continued healing with occasional difficult periods, especially around anniversaries, holidays, or major life events.

Year 2 and beyond: Many people experience significant improvement, though occasional triggers may still cause temporary symptoms.

Remember that everyone's timeline is different, and there's no "right" way to experience withdrawal. Some people have intense symptoms for a short time; others have milder symptoms that last longer.

The No-Contact Principle

The most effective way to break a trauma bond is to implement complete no-contact with your abuser. This means no phone calls, no texts, no emails, no social media contact, no "checking up" on them, no personal stalking, and no contact through mutual friends or family members.

Why No-Contact is Essential:

It stops intermittent reinforcement. Every time you have contact with your abuser, even negative contact, you're feeding the addiction. Your brain gets a hit of the chemicals it's craving, which resets your withdrawal timeline and strengthens the bond.

It allows your brain to heal. Just like a drug addict needs to stop using drugs for their brain to heal, you need to stop having contact with your abuser for your brain to break the addiction.

It prevents manipulation. The sound of the Cat's voice, his scent, his touch—think you're strong enough to resist, Sis? Your abuser will likely try to pull you back in when they realize you're serious about leaving. No-contact prevents them from using their *tried-and-true* manipulation tactics to weaken your resolve.

It gives you space to think clearly. When you're in regular contact with your abuser, your brain is constantly in survival mode. No-contact gives you the mental space to process what happened and make decisions based on reality rather than fear and terror.

Implementing No-Contact:

Honey, block them everywhere! Block their phone number, email address, and all social media accounts. Ask friends and family not to share information about you with them or about them with you.

Remove reminders. Put away photos, gifts, and anything else that reminds you of them. You don't have to throw these things away forever, but remove them from your immediate environment.

Change your routines. If you used to go to certain places together, avoid those places for a while. Change your routines to minimize the chance of running into them.

Prepare for contact attempts. They will likely try to contact you, especially in the beginning. Prepare yourself mentally for this and have a plan for how you'll respond (or not respond).

Get support. Tell your support system about your no-contact decision and ask for their help in maintaining it. Having accountability makes it much easier to stick to your commitment.

Managing Cravings and Urges

Even with no-contact in place, you will experience intense cravings to reach out to your abuser. These cravings are a normal part of breaking any addiction, and they will pass if you don't act on them.

Craving Management Strategies:

Surf the urge. Cravings come in waves that build, peak, and then subside. Instead of fighting the craving, acknowledge it and ride it out like a surfer riding a wave. Be honest with yourself, "I'm having a craving right now, I want to text him so bad. This will pass."

Use the 24-hour rule. When you feel an intense urge to contact them, commit to waiting 24 hours. Often, the urge will have passed by then. If it hasn't, commit to another 24 hours.

Distract yourself. Have a list of activities ready for when cravings hit: call a friend, go for a walk, take a bath, watch a movie, clean your house, exercise, or engage in a hobby.

Write a letter you don't send. Sometimes you need to get your thoughts and feelings out on paper or on-screen. Write them a letter saying everything you want to say, then delete it or burn it.

Remember why you left. One of the best pieces of relationship advice I ever got was: "Remember the bad times." Keep a list of all the reasons you ended the relationship. When your emotions start romanticizing the good times, read this list to remind yourself of the reality.

Practice self-care. Cravings are often worse when you're tired, hungry, lonely, or stressed. Take care of your basic needs to reduce the intensity of cravings.

Pray and fast. Women of faith, disciples of Jesus Christ—get in your Bible, pray, and turn down your plate. This was my go-to when the cravings began to suffocate me. Our petitions to God will never go unanswered, and fasting has a way of killing our fleshly desires and stumbling blocks in ways that no-contact alone cannot.

Cat Tactics Decoded

The Hoover Maneuver: Named after the vacuum cleaner, this is when the Cat tries to "suck" you back into the relationship after you've left. They might suddenly become the person you always wanted them to be, promising change, declaring their love, or creating a crisis that requires your help.

The Trauma Bond Exploitation: The Cat understands that you're bonded to them and will use this against you. They might say things like "You know you can't live without me, we're good together" or "No one will ever love you like I do" to exploit your attachment.

The Intermittent Contact: Even after you've established no-contact, the Cat might try to maintain the trauma bond through sporadic contact—a random text, a sneaky social media like, or an unexpected visit. Any contact feeds the addiction and keeps you hooked.

Mouse Traps

The "Just Friends" Trap: Ma'am, don't convince yourself that you can maintain a friendship with your abuser because you've "moved past" the romantic relationship. Trauma bonds don't respect relationship labels, and any contact will likely reactivate the addiction. Be your own best friend first.

The Closure Trap: You believe you need one final conversation to get closure or to tell them how they hurt you. Did the Cat understand, empathize, or change the last time you said these same words? Closure comes from within, not from them, and seeking it often leads to getting pulled back in.

The Gradual Contact Trap: You think you can slowly reduce contact instead of going no-contact immediately. This is like trying to quit smoking by gradually reducing cigarettes from 5 to 4 per day—it rarely works and often prolongs the addiction.

The Exception Trap: You make exceptions to no-contact for "emergencies," special occasions, or because you feel sorry for them. Every exception *re-glues* the trauma bond and makes it harder to break free.

Rebuilding Your Identity

As you break the trauma bond, you'll need to rebuild your sense of self that was lost or compromised during the relationship. Trauma bonding often involves losing yourself in the other person, so recovery involves rediscovering who you are apart from them.

Reconnecting with Your Authentic Self:

- Remember who you were before the relationship; who does God say you are?
- Reconnect with old friends and interests you abandoned
- Explore new hobbies and activities that bring you joy
- Practice making decisions based on your own preferences, not theirs
- Spend time alone to hear your own thoughts and feel your own feelings
- Set goals that have nothing to do with relationships, romance, or them

Building New, Healthy Relationships:

- Invest in friendships and family relationships
- Consider getting a pet if that appeals to you
- Join groups or communities based on your interests
- Work with a therapist who understands trauma bonding
- Practice healthy attachment in safe relationships

Breaking a trauma bond is one of the hardest things you'll ever do, but it's also one of the most important. It's the difference between being a prisoner of your past and being free to create your future. It's the difference between surviving and thriving.

Grieving this *strange glue* is not optional. You can't skip it, rush it, or intellectualize your way through it. You have to feel it. Allow yourself to cry, to feel angry, to feel sad, to feel confused. These emotions are all part of the healing process.

Don't judge yourself for grieving someone who hurt you. It's normal to miss even toxic relationships because they met some of your needs, even if they also caused you harm. You can grieve the loss while still knowing that leaving was the right choice.

In the next chapter, we'll explore the crucial topic of forgiveness - both forgiving yourself for what you didn't know and couldn't control, and the complex process of forgiving someone who terrorized your soul. We'll discover how forgiveness becomes the key that unlocks the final chains keeping you bound to your past.

For now, remember: the pain of breaking free from a trauma bond is temporary, but the freedom you'll gain is forever.

11

Chapter 11: Forgiving Yourself (And the Cat)

"Be kind and compassionate to one another, forgiving each other, just as in Christ God forgave you." - Ephesians 4:32

Forgiveness might be the most misunderstood concept in the entire healing journey. The moment you mention forgiveness in the context of abuse, people either shut down completely or start spouting platitudes about "letting go" and "moving on"—but doing so with such simplicity reveals that they've never walked this particular path of pain.

Let me be clear from the start: forgiveness is not about excusing what happened to you. It's not about pretending the abuse wasn't bad, or that the Cat didn't mean to hurt you, or that you should just forget about it and move on. Forgiveness is also not about reconciliation or giving someone permission to hurt you again.

Forgiveness, at its core, is about freedom. Your freedom. It's about releasing yourself from the prison of bitterness, resentment, and the exhausting burden of carrying someone else's debt. As a woman of faith, for me it's about choosing to let God handle the justice I deserve while I focus on the healing and wholeness I need.

That being said, this chapter will challenge you. It will ask you to consider forgiveness not as weakness, but as the ultimate act of the "C" in B.I.T.C.H.—courage. Will forgiveness require you to give up your right to justice? No. But are you willing to trust God to handle justice better than you ever could? The ask is not to excuse the inexcusable, but to refuse to let the inexcusable continue to poison your life.

Let's dive in and explore two types of forgiveness that are essential for your complete healing: forgiving yourself for what you didn't know (maybe refused to see, and now regret), and forgiving the Cat for the emotional terrorism they inflicted on your soul. Both are necessary. Both can be difficult. Both are possible with God's help.

The Burden You Were Never Meant to Carry

Imagine lifting a two-ton rock off of someone's shoulders, all while struggling with a four-ton boulder on yours. When it comes to forgiveness, we really need to talk about how difficult it is to free someone else from the very chains that keep us bound. So before we talk about forgiving anyone else, we need to address the heaviest burden you're carrying right now: the weight of shame, self-blame, self-condemnation, and self-punishment for what happened to you.

If you're like me, you blame yourself for not seeing the red flags sooner, ignoring the red flags you did see, for staying too long, for believing their lies, for not being stronger, for not knowing your worth, for not protecting yourself better. Does any of that sound familiar? You carry shame for the ways you compromised your values, the times you lost yourself, the dreams put on the back burner, the moments you became someone you didn't recognize.

You've punished yourself relentlessly with thoughts like "I should have known better," "I was so stupid," "I wasted so many years."

Or perhaps, the Big Joker of all thoughts: "He's right. I was a dumb bitch!" Let's face it—nothing sucks worse than the Cat actually being right about some of the dumb decisions we made.

Here's what I need you to understand: you are carrying a burden that was never yours to bear. You are taking responsibility for someone else's choices, someone else's cruelty, and someone else's decision to harm you. You are punishing yourself for being human in an inhumane situation. That stops now.

What You Need to Forgive Yourself For

For not knowing what you didn't know. You didn't know about narcissistic abuse, trauma bonding, or manipulation tactics. I didn't know that all the words and gestures of love and devotion were love bombing tactics to manipulate my emotions. You didn't know that love could be weaponized or how your kindness could be exploited. You operated from your own heart, assuming others had the same capacity for love and empathy.

For not being stronger than you were. You weren't weak for staying. You weren't dumb for believing them. You weren't weak for hoping they would change. You were human, and humans are wired for connection, hope, and love. Your capacity for these Beautiful things was used against you, but that doesn't make you weak.

For the survival strategies you used. You did what you had to do to survive. If you people-pleased, if you walked on eggshells, if you lost yourself trying to keep the peace, if you gave your last, if you smiled for the camera while weeping inside, you were adapting to an impossible situation. These weren't character flaws; they were survival mechanisms.

For the time you "lost." You didn't lose those years; you lived them. You learned things about yourself, about relationships, about Tenacity and Courage that you couldn't have learned any other way. For me, thirty-two of my best years feels like an entire generation of time—because it was. I had to resolve that those years weren't wasted; they were the foundation for the wisdom and strength I have today.

For not leaving sooner or for being "left". You left when you were ready to leave, when you had the resources to leave, when you finally understood what you were dealing with. Leaving an abusive relationship is one of the most dangerous and complex decisions a person can make. And sometimes, that decision isn't made by you, it's made *for* you. Some of you are like me and have to forgive yourself for allowing yourself to get "left", discarded, or abandoned by the Cat. It's an added insult to years of narcissistic injury you have endured that now requires you to be gentle with yourself.

The Radical Act of Self-Compassion

Self-forgiveness isn't just about releasing guilt and shame. It's about extending to yourself the same compassion you would offer to any woman who had been through what you've been through.

Self-Compassion Practices

Talk to yourself like you would talk to someone you love. When the self-critical voice starts up, ask yourself: "Would I say this to my best friend who's hurting? Would I talk to my daughter this way after she's experienced emotional terrorism?" Then speak to yourself with the same kindness you would offer them.

Acknowledge your humanity. Can you join the rest of the human race and be okay with *not* being perfect? Perfection is the one thing we were never created to be. You made the best decisions you could with the information, resources, and strength you had at the time. That's all any human would do.

Honor your survival. Instead of focusing on what you "should have" done differently, celebrate what you did do. You survived! You endured. You found the strength to leave. You found the Courage to keep going. You're here, reading this, working on your healing—and that's extraordinary.

Practice radically simple acceptance. Accept that what happened, happened. Simple as that. Accept that you can't change the past. Accept that you are exactly where you need to be in your healing journey. Acceptance doesn't mean approval; it means stopping the exhausting fight against reality and truth.

The Misunderstood Gift of Forgiving the Cat

Now we come to the part that might make you want to throw this book across the room: forgiving the person who terrorized you. Lord Jesus! Before you do, hear me out. This isn't about them. This is about you. Cliché? No, truth.

Forgiveness is not a gift you give to your abuser. It's a gift-wrapped *key* for yourself that unlocks a wealth of freedom you can't imagine right now. It's not about setting them free; it's about setting yourself free. It's about taking back the power and control that their toxic behavior had over your life—even when they're no longer in your life.

What Forgiveness Is NOT:

- Excusing or minimizing what they did to you
- Pretending the pain wasn't painful
- Giving them permission to hurt you again
- Reconciling or restoring the relationship
- Trusting them or allowing them back into your life
- Forgetting what happened
- Bypassing your anger or grief
- Rushing your healing process through an express lane

What Forgiveness IS:

- Releasing your right to punish them and trusting God with justice
- Choosing to stop rehearsing their wrongs in your mind
- Freeing yourself from the burden of bitterness, resentment, and revenge
- Refusing to let their actions continue to poison your present
- Trusting God to handle what you cannot handle
- Choosing your own healing over their punishment
- Breaking the chains that keep you connected to your abuser

The Biblical Foundation for Forgiveness

For disciples of Christ, God's Word is clear about forgiveness, and it's not optional. Jesus said, "If you forgive other people when they sin against you, your heavenly Father will also forgive you. But if you do not forgive others their sins, your Father will not forgive your sins" (Matthew 6:14-15).

This isn't because God is trying to make your life harder. It's because He knows that unforgiveness is a poison that destroys the person carrying it. He knows that bitterness and resentment manipulated by the *twisting* of Leviathan will eat away at your soul, steal your joy, and prevent you from experiencing the fullness of life God has planned for you.

The Benefits of Forgiveness for You:

Freedom from the past. When you forgive, you stop being defined by what was done to you. There's a benefit to not sitting in the "mess" of the past, regurgitating the pain. You can become defined by how you *choose* to respond to what was done to you.

Emotional liberation. Anger, bitterness, and resentment are exhausting emotions to carry. Forgiveness frees up that emotional energy for healing, growth, goals, and joy.

Physical health. Research shows that forgiveness reduces stress, lowers blood pressure, improves immune function, clears skin, and reduces the risk of heart disease. Unforgiveness literally tarnishes your Beauty and makes you sick.

Spiritual freedom. Unforgiveness creates a barrier between you and God. For the road ahead, you need God's very present help. When you forgive, you remove that barrier and open yourself to receive God's healing, peace, and blessings.

Breaking generational patterns. Do resentment, unforgiveness, or long-held grudges that no one can clearly articulate run in your family? If so, is it time to break this family tradition? When you choose forgiveness over bitterness, you break cycles of hurt, offense, and revenge that could affect your children and their children.

The Benefits of Forgiveness for the Cat:

No, you didn't wake up today wondering, *how can I benefit the one who broke me?* While forgiveness is primarily for your benefit, it can also release the Cat from the spiritual bondage of your unforgiveness. Unforgiveness can transform you into a special kind of feline who's drunk with holding her abuser hostage—is that who you are? If not, know that forgiveness doesn't remove consequences, but it does:

Shine a light on the path to their own conviction and repentance. Sometimes our unforgiveness actually enables someone to stay in denial about their behavior. When we release them, God can deal with their heart and expose the true intent of their actions to them.

Release them to face the natural consequences of their actions. When we're focused on punishing someone, we sometimes interfere with the natural consequences God would allow. Forgiveness gets us out of the way so God can work.

Position you as an "overcomer" to watch. As forgiveness brings healing and restoration, people are watching—including the Cat. "How did she heal?" "How does she look better than when we were together?" "I took everything I could from her, and now she has more!" You will become a living, breathing testimony of what God can do.

The Process of Forgiveness

Forgiveness is not a feeling; it's a *decision*. You don't have to feel like forgiving to choose forgiveness. In fact, you probably won't feel like forgiving at first, and that's normal and okay. Forgiveness is an act of the will that often precedes the feeling and willingness. Here are some phases you will cycle through on the road to forgiveness:

Acknowledge the Debt

Be honest about what was done to you. Don't minimize it, excuse it, or pretend it wasn't that bad. Make a list if you need to. Acknowledge the full extent of the harm that was done.

Feel Your Feelings

You can't forgive what you haven't fully felt. Allow yourself to feel the anger, the hurt, the betrayal, the grief. These emotions are valid and necessary. Don't rush through them or try to over-spiritualize them away.

Choose to Release

These are the moments of decision. You choose to release your right to punish this person. You might need to make this choice multiple times as feelings resurface.

Pray for Them

Jesus said to pray for those who persecute you (Matthew 5:44). This doesn't mean praying that they'll get away with what they did. It means praying for their salvation, their healing, their transformation. This is often the hardest part, but it's also the most powerful.

Trust God with Justice

"Do not take revenge, my dear friends, but leave room for God's wrath, for it is written: 'It is mine to avenge; I will repay,' says the Lord" (Romans 12:19). God saw what was done to you—even the stuff you don't know about. He cares about justice even more than you do. Trust Him to handle it in His way and His timing.

How To Tell When the Forgiveness Process is Over

Is this even a thing? Is forgiveness ever over? Right now, when you think about the magnitude of pain and damage on the table to be forgiven, it seems like this will be a lifelong process—"I'm never getting out of forgiveness jail!"

In some ways, Sis, you're absolutely right! I've experienced a forgiveness journey with the Cat that comes in waves, where you meet new triggers or discover new information that sends you back to the altar of forgiveness like you forgot something.

While you may or may not experience an official forgiveness "finish line" complete with checkerboard flags, there are some strong indicators that forgiveness is approaching full bloom in your heart. This happens when:

You can reference it without reliving it. When you recount your season of emotional terrorism, how you communicate what happened provides forgiveness cues. When we *reference* a past event, we simply state that "it happened". We know we're *reliving* a situation with "it happened to me", and it evokes all of its negative energy and emotions.

Revenge, payback, or retaliation become non-issues. When you honestly and truthfully wish the Cat the best, when you hope no harm comes to them, when they no longer have to pay penance for what they did, your forgiveness is reaching a Beautiful milestone.

You understand the difference between buried pain and forgiveness. I remember my carefully crafted mask of "that doesn't bother me anymore" and "I'm really not phased, I'm over it." All lies! Hiding unforgiveness behind denial only prolongs your pain and stunts your healing. When you do the forgiveness work to honestly let it go, the pain will no longer claw its way back to the surface.

You fully accept that God loves the Cat as much as He loves you. Sometimes it's hard to comprehend how God can love someone who did something so horrible to us. When the forgiveness journey begins, we deem ourselves "higher, or better" than the person who offended us. But, as we walk through forgiveness over time, our sense of self in relation to the Cat miraculously *evens out*. We're able to own that we ourselves have done wrong and offended others, and that we need God's love and forgiveness too.

When Forgiveness Feels Impossible

There will be days when forgiveness feels impossible, when the hurt is too fresh, when the injustice feels too great. On those days, remember:

Forgiveness is a process, not a one-time event. You might need to choose forgiveness daily, or even multiple times a day. That doesn't mean you're failing; it means you're human.

You don't have to feel it to choose it. Forgiveness is an act of obedience to God, not a feeling you have to manufacture. Choose it even when you don't feel it, and trust that the feelings will follow.

God will help you. You don't have to forgive in your own strength. Ask God to help you forgive, to give you the grace and power to release what you cannot release on your own.

It's okay to start small. If you can't forgive everything at once, start with something small. Forgive them for one specific incident, or for one day, or for one hour. Build your forgiveness muscle gradually.

Cat Tactics Decoded

The Forgiveness Manipulation: The Cat may demand forgiveness from you while showing no genuine remorse or changed behavior. They might use your faith against you, saying things like "Christians are supposed to forgive" or "If you really loved me, you'd forgive me." Remember that forgiveness doesn't require the relationship to remain intact.

The False Repentance: The Cat might offer what seems like an apology or acknowledgment of wrongdoing, but it's actually manipulation designed to get you to drop your boundaries or return to the relationship. True repentance involves genuine remorse, taking full responsibility, and changed behavior over time—not a forgiveness performance.

The Forgiveness Pressure: Others might pressure you, saying things like "You need to forgive and move on" or "Holding onto anger is only hurting you." While forgiveness is important, it must not be rushed, forced, or faked. Forgive in God's timing, with His help, not based on others' expectations.

Mouse Traps

The Premature Forgiveness Trap: You try to forgive before you've fully processed the hurt, thinking this will speed up your healing. Premature forgiveness often leads to spiritual bypassing and incomplete healing.

The Feeling-Based Forgiveness Trap: You wait to feel *forgiving* before you choose to forgive. Forgiveness is a decision that often precedes the feeling, not the other way around.

The Reconciliation Trap: You believe that forgiving someone means you have to reconcile with them or allow them back into your life. Forgiveness and reconciliation are two different things. Reconciliation requires repentance, changed behavior, and rebuilt trust.

The Perfect Forgiveness Trap: You expect to forgive once and never feel angry or hurt about it again. Forgiveness is often a process that requires multiple choices over time, especially for deep wounds.

Living in the Freedom of Forgiveness

When you choose forgiveness - both for yourself and for the Cat - you step into a freedom unlike any you've ever experienced before. You're no longer defined by what was done to you. You're no longer carrying the exhausting burden of someone else's debt. You're no longer giving your abuser power over your present and future.

Does this mean you'll never feel hurt or angry again? No. Feelings will feel. You will remember things. The difference now is that you've chosen to let God handle the justice while you focus on the healing.

You've chosen to break the cycle of hurt and revenge. You've chosen to be defined by your response to adversity rather than by the adversity itself. You've chosen freedom over bondage, healing over bitterness, hope over despair. And each one of these decisions will pay off in your favor.

In the next chapter, we'll explore how to reclaim your identity and rebuild your sense of self after it's been systematically dismantled. We'll discover who you really are beneath the layers of trauma and conditioning, and we'll learn how to live from that authentic place of strength and Beauty.

For now, remember: forgiveness is not weakness. It's the ultimate act of strength and Courage to walk out of an open cell. It's choosing to love yourself enough to set yourself free.

12

Chapter 12: The Beautiful Truth About You

"Your workmanship is marvelous—how well I know it." - Psalm 139:14

You've spent so long seeing yourself through the Cat's distorted lens that you've forgotten who *you* really are. You've internalized their criticism, accepted their assessment of your worth, and believed their narrative about your inadequacy. You've been living as a refugee in your own life, displaced by an emotional terrorist from your true identity and convinced that you deserve whatever scraps of affection they're willing to throw your way.

But here's the Beautiful truth about you they never wanted you to discover: you are not who they said you were. You never were.

The woman reading these words right now is not the broken, desperate, too-hard-to-love creature the Cat painted you to be. You are not too sensitive, too hard, too insecure, too needy, too loud, too plain, too difficult, or too much. You are not the sum of your worst moments or the collection of your deepest trauma wounds. You are not defined by what was done to you or what you *allowed* to be done to you.

You are a masterpiece that has been vandalized, not destroyed. You are a diamond that has been buried under layers of lies, but you haven't been transformed into coal. You are a song that has been temporarily paused, not permanently muted. And, it's time for you to remember the melody of who you were created to be.

The Grand Identity Theft

Before you can reclaim your true identity, let's decode how it was stolen in the first place. Identity theft in abusive relationships isn't a single dramatic event. It's a gradual erosion that happens so slowly you don't notice until you wake up one day and don't recognize the person staring back at you in the mirror.

The Cat didn't just attack your behavior or criticize your choices. They systematically dismantled your sense of self, piece by piece, until you began to see yourself through their eyes instead of God's eyes. They convinced you that their opinion of you was more accurate than your own experience with yourself. They made you believe that their assessment of your worth was more valid than the One who *knit you together* in your mother's womb.

This identity theft began with subtle suggestions that you weren't quite good enough as you were. Maybe you were called something like, "too emotional, too independent, too trusting, too naive." These labels weren't presented as cruel criticisms but as helpful observations from someone who "loved you enough to tell you the truth." They positioned themselves as your personal improvement coach, generously offering to help you become a better version of yourself. And let's remember, the Cat has some endearing qualities, abilities, and personality traits of their own that make them very influential and admirable. Perhaps you initially thought, "Maybe he's on to something. He's probably right."

Over time, these suggestions became demands. You needed to change your communication style, your social circle, your interests, your goals, your dreams, your hair. Nothing about you was quite right. Everything needed adjustment, modification, or complete overhaul. You began to see yourself as a perpetual work in progress—always falling short of their standards, always needing to try harder to earn their approval, always chasing a moving goal post.

The final stage of identity theft was when you began to police yourself. You no longer needed the Cat to tell you that you were wrong, inadequate, or disappointing. Now, he's the ventriloquist and you're the puppet. You had internalized his voice so deeply that it became your own inner critic. You started seeing yourself through their lens automatically, judging yourself by *their* standards, and finding yourself lacking before they even had a chance to point out your failures.

If you're like me, the chilling *irony* of this stage that made you crazy is the Cat saying, "You've got to be more confident. Why are you so hard on yourself? " (Huh? Wonder why.) "Do you see how I carry myself? Not a dime in my pocket, and I'll be the most confident man in the room." Now you feel bad and confused for internalizing their beliefs, subconsciously thinking that changing yourself would please them.

This, Ma'am, is how someone can steal your identity without ever touching your credit cards or social security number. They simply convince you that who you are isn't good enough, and then they offer to tell you who you should be instead. Before you know it, you're living someone else's version of your life, trying to become someone else's bad idea of who you should be until they flip the script and send you in yet another direction.

Self-Worth vs. Assigned Value

One of the most crucial distinctions you need to understand is the difference between self-worth and assigned value. Self-worth is inherent, unchanging, and comes from your identity as a beloved daughter of God. Assigned value is external, fluctuating, and comes from other people's opinions, assessments, and treatment of you.

The Cat operates entirely in the realm of assigned value. They position themselves as the authority on your worth, the judge of your adequacy, the arbiter of your value. They make you believe that your worth was contingent upon their approval and subject to their ever-changing standards. They convince you that you had to earn love, deserve respect, and prove your value through your performance.

This is a lie that once again goes all the way back to the Garden of Eden. The serpent convinced Eve that God was withholding something from her, that she needed to do something to become more than who she already was. The truth is that she was already enough. She was already loved and provided for.

She was already valuable. She didn't need to earn what she already possessed.

Your self-worth isn't based on how well you please, how perfectly you perform, or how successfully you meet someone else's expectations. Your worth isn't determined by your productivity, your appearance, your achievements, or your ability to make and keep someone else happy. Your worth isn't even determined by your mistakes, your failures, your weaknesses, or your worst moments.

Your worth is based on one thing and one thing alone: the fact that you are fearfully and wonderfully made by a God who doesn't make mistakes. Psalm 139:14 isn't a suggestion or a nice sentiment. It's a declaration of truth about your Beautiful identity. You are not an accident, a mistake, or a disappointment to your Creator. God looked at you and said, "It was good!" You are His workmanship, created in Christ Jesus for good works that He prepared in advance for you to walk in (Ephesians 2:10).

This worth cannot be increased by someone's approval or decreased by someone's rejection. It cannot be earned through good behavior or lost through bad choices. It cannot be given by another person or taken away by their abuse. It simply is, because you are, and you are because God chose to create you exactly as you are for this exact moment in time.

Reclaiming Your God-Given Dignity

Remember the *thief* in Chapter 9? You've been robbed of your dignity. Dignity is different from worth, though they're closely related. While worth is about your inherent value, dignity is about how that value should be *honored* and *protected*. Dignity is about the respect you deserve simply by virtue of being a worthy human, the treatment you have a right to expect, and the boundaries that should never be crossed.

The Cat violates your dignity repeatedly and systematically. They treat you as less than human, speak to you in ways that no person should ever be spoken to, e.g., "Dumb bitch!", and cross boundaries that should have been sacred. They convince you that this treatment is normal, deserved, or even loving. They make you believe that accepting disrespect is evidence of your maturity, that tolerating abuse is proof of your commitment, and that enduring cruelty is a demonstration of your love.

This is not love or piety. This is not what you were created to accept.

You were created to be treated with honor, respect, and kindness. You were created to be spoken to with gentleness, listened to with attention, and valued for who you are, not just what you can provide. You were created to have your boundaries respected, your feelings acknowledged, and your needs considered important.

The fact that someone violated your dignity doesn't mean you don't deserve respect. The fact that someone treated you poorly doesn't mean you're not worthy of better treatment. The fact that someone convinced you to accept less than you deserve doesn't mean that's all you're worth.

Reclaiming your dignity starts with recognizing that you have it. It's not something you need to earn or prove. It's something you possess by virtue of being made in the image of God. It's something that should be honored by others and protected by you.

This means you have the right to be treated with respect, even when someone disagrees with you. Your feelings have the right to be acknowledged, even when someone doesn't understand them. You have the right to set boundaries, even when someone doesn't like them, and the right to say no, even when someone wants you to say yes.

With these rights come personal responsibility. You also have the responsibility to honor your own dignity. This means refusing to accept treatment that degrades you, speaking to yourself with the same kindness you would show a friend, and making choices that reflect your true worth rather than your wounded self-perception.

Taking Inventory of Your Strength

One of the most damaging lies the Cat told you was that you were weak. They convinced you that your sensitivity was weakness, your kindness was naivety, your forgiveness was foolishness, and your love was desperation. They made you believe that your very best qualities were actually character flaws that needed to be corrected or hidden.

The truth is exactly the opposite. The qualities the Cat criticized in you are actually evidence of your strength, not your weakness. Let's take an honest inventory of what it really took to survive what you've been through.

Your Sensitivity is Strength: The Cat called you "too sensitive" because your emotional awareness threatened their ability to manipulate you. Sensitivity isn't weakness; it's emotional intelligence. It's the ability to perceive what others miss, to feel what others ignore, and to respond to the emotional undercurrents that shape every human interaction. Your sensitivity is what made you aware that something was wrong long before you had words to describe it.

Your Compassion is Courage: The Cat criticized your compassion for others because it interfered with their agenda to make everything about them. But compassion requires tremendous courage. It takes strength to feel someone else's pain, to care about their well-being (even when they don't care about yours), and to maintain your heart's softness in a world that often rewards hardness.

Your Loyalty is Leadership: The Cat exploited your loyalty while simultaneously criticizing it as weakness or stupidity. But loyalty is actually a form of leadership. It's the ability to see potential in people and situations, to commit to something beyond yourself, and to persevere through difficulties that would cause others to quit. Your loyalty isn't evidence of your desperation; it's evidence of your character.

Your Forgiveness is Freedom: The Cat demanded your forgiveness while offering none in return, then mocked you for being "too forgiving" when it served their purposes. What does that look like? "Bay, I forgive you. Forgive yourself. Don't let the enemy win and break up our family because you cheated. We can beat this together." "What I did must not have hurt that bad—you still forgave me, you're still here, aren't you?" Forgiveness isn't an act of weakness; it's one of the strongest things a human being can do. It takes incredible strength to release resentment, to choose healing over hatred, and to refuse to let someone else's behavior poison your heart.

Your Hope is Heroism: The Cat mocked your hope, calling it delusion or denial. But hope in the face of disappointment isn't naivety; it's heroism. It takes tremendous courage to keep believing in love when you've been shown cruelty, to keep trusting in goodness when you've experienced evil, and to keep moving forward when everything in you wants to give up. These are the seeds to becoming your own hero.

Your Survival is Success: Most importantly, you need to recognize that your very survival is evidence of your strength. You endured emotional and psychological warfare that would have broken many people. You maintained your sanity in an environment designed to make you crazy. "Damned if you do, damned if you don't" treatment is a weapon of mass destruction to a heart that wants to succeed.

So, you didn't just survive; you survived with your heart intact, and your ability to love still functioning. Your hope refused to die, so your faith kept breathing. That's not weakness, sis. That's miraculous strength.

Mouse Traps

The Improvement Trap: You believed that if you could just fix your "flaws" and become the person the Cat wanted you to be, the relationship would improve. This trap kept you focused on changing yourself instead of recognizing that the problem was their treatment of you, not your response to their treatment.

The Gratitude Trap: You felt guilty for being unhappy because the Cat *occasionally* showed you kindness or because your situation could have been worse. This trap prevented you from acknowledging the full extent of the damage being done to your emotional and spiritual well-being. You have the right to feel sadness, anger, or disappointment—even when the Cat offers moments of kindness. Your feelings cannot be bought or erased.

The Strength Denial: You minimized your own strength and resilience because acknowledging how much you had endured would have meant acknowledging how badly you were being treated. It was easier to see yourself as weak than to face the reality of your situation or hold the Cat accountable.

The Worth Negotiation: You believed that your worth was something that could be debated, earned, or proven rather than something that simply existed. You were stuck in battle cycles, fighting for your worth to be seen, understood, and honored to no avail. This trap kept you trying to convince the Cat of your value instead of you simply knowing it without the need to justify, argue, defend, or explain it.

Stepping Into Your True Identity

Reclaiming your identity isn't about becoming someone new. It's about remembering who you've always been underneath the layers of lies, criticism, and manipulation. God can put the pieces of you back together. Like reconnecting broken bones, dust off those dreams that were buried, rekindle the passions that were extinguished, and reconnect with the woman God created you to be.

This process takes time, patience, and tremendous self-compassion. You've been living in exile from yourself for so long, fighting through the cat-and-mouse game, that coming home to your true identity might feel foreign at first. You might not trust your own perceptions, your own feelings, or your own judgment. You might feel guilty for taking up space, asking for what you need, or believing that you deserve better.

These feelings are normal and temporary. They're the residue of psychological abuse, not the truth about who you are. Every time you choose to honor your own feelings, every time you set and keep a boundary, every time you speak the truth, every time you treat yourself with kindness, you're taking another step toward reclaiming your authentic self.

Remember that the Cat's opinion of you was never the truth. It was a projection of their own insecurities, a reflection of their own brokenness, and a manifestation of the spiritual darkness operating through them. Their assessment of your worth says nothing about you and everything about the condition of their own heart.

You are not too much. You are not too little. You are not too broken to be loved or too damaged to be healed. You are not a mistake, an accident, a failure, or a disappointment. You are exactly who God intended you to be, and you are exactly who the world needs you to be.

In the next chapter, we'll explore the moment of awakening when a smart woman finally says, "enough is enough." Are you feeling like you're almost there? Let's examine how clarity emerges from crisis and how to nurture that awakening into lasting change, even when everything around you tries to pull you back into denial.

As always, hold this truth close: you are fearfully and wonderfully made, and that has never changed, no matter what anyone has told you or done to you.

13

Chapter 13: The Intelligent Woman's Awakening

"Then you will know the truth, and the truth will set you free." - John 8:32

There comes a moment in every Intelligent woman's journey through emotional terrorism when something shifts. It might happen in an instant, like a lightning bolt of clarity cutting through years of confusion. Or, it might unfold slowly, like dawn breaking after the longest argumentative night of your life. But when it happens, you know. You finally, undeniably, unshakably know that this is not love, this is not healthy, and this kind of "normal" is not what you were created to endure.

This is your awakening.

It's the moment when your Intelligence finally overrides unwise hope. When your intuition finally drowns out their gaslighting. When your self-preservation finally outweighs your people-pleasing. When your truth finally becomes louder than their lies.

For some women, this awakening comes after a particularly brutal attack on their character, their sanity, or their safety. For others, it comes in a quiet moment when they realize they can't remember the last time they felt genuinely happy. For others still, it comes when they see their children beginning to normalize the dysfunction in the home or when they catch a glimpse of themselves in the mirror and don't recognize the hollow-eyed, aged stranger staring back.

Sis, however your awakening arrives, it's sacred. It's the moment when your heart finally says what your soul has been trying to tell you for months or years: enough is enough.

The Anatomy of Rock Bottom

Rock bottom isn't always dramatic. It's not always a single catastrophic event that makes the evening news or sends you to the emergency room. Sometimes, rock bottom is simply the quiet realization that you've lost yourself so completely that you're not sure you'll ever find your way back to who you used to be.

Rock bottom might be the morning you wake up and realize you've been walking on eggshells for so long that you've forgotten what it feels like to move freely through your own life. It might be the moment you catch yourself rehearsing a simple conversation in your head, trying to predict every possible way they might twist your words against you.

It might be when you realize you've stopped sharing good news because their envious response always manages to diminish your joy. Or when you notice that you've started lying to friends and family about your relationship because the truth is too exhausting to explain and too painful to admit.

For many smart women, rock bottom is the devastating realization that they've become complicit in their own destruction. They've participated in the gaslighting by doubting their own perceptions. They've enabled the abuse by making excuses for inexcusable behavior. They've betrayed themselves by staying silent when their soul was screaming for them to speak up.

Some women never find their rock bottom and have to borrow God's. Let's decode this. Every time rock bottom tried to present itself to me, I misused the "T" in B.I.T.C.H.—I would Tenaciously find ways to keep digging, keep trying, keep forgiving, keep hoping. Rock bottom for me happened when my last shovel hit God's iron slab of "enough is enough". God had grown weary of the cat-and-mouse game and had to yank my tail out kicking, screaming, and looking back. "I know the police just left the house after he choked me, and he's probably headed to 'her' house (and did), but how long do you think counseling and therapy will take to heal us this time?" Funny how God spoke to me in my own voice: "Ma'am, this is your exit. Take my hand, come with Me, this is where you get off. This toxic relationship is over. It's time for you to heal."

I was devastated, crushed. The woman who prided herself on her Intelligence, her strength, her ability to solve problems and fix situations, suddenly sees that she's been in covenant "by herself", using all of those gifts to maintain a relationship that was slowly killing her spirit. She's been applying her considerable talents and resources to the wrong problem, trying to fix someone who didn't want to be fixed while neglecting the one person she actually had the power to save: herself.

Here's what you need to understand about rock bottom: it's not a place of defeat. It's a place of clarity. Initially, sis? You better believe after three decades, I wanted to go and die from the pain and shame. But this place of crippling revelation would become my genesis—the place where I'd eventually be reborn. Rock bottom is actually solid ground, the first firm foundation you've stood on in years. It's the place where you finally stop digging and start climbing.

The pain of rock bottom is real, but it's also purposeful. It's your soul's way of saying, "We cannot go any lower. We will not accept any less. We refuse to live like this for one more minute." Rock bottom is where your survival instincts finally override your people-pleasing programming.

Clarity Through Crisis

Crisis has a way of *burning away* everything that isn't essential, leaving only what matters most. When you're in the middle of emotional terrorism, it's easy to get lost in the daily drama, the constant chaos, the endless cycle of conflict and temporary reconciliation. But crisis cuts through all of that noise and forces you to see the situation with startling clarity.

In crisis, you can no longer afford the luxury of denial, or pretend that things will get better if you just try harder, love more, or give them one more chance. Crisis demands honesty, and honesty reveals truths that hope has been hiding.

You might see clearly for the first time that their promises of change have been empty words designed to buy them more time to continue their destructive patterns or suck your resources dry. You might recognize that their apologies have been manipulation tactics rather than genuine remorse. You might also realize that their love has always been conditional, contingent on your willingness to accept unacceptable treatment.

Crisis also reveals your own strength in ways that ordinary circumstances never did. When everything is falling apart, you discover what you're really made of. You find reserves of courage you didn't know you possessed. You access wisdom that had been buried under years of self-doubt. You connect with an inner voice that had been silenced by their constant criticism and control.

The clarity that comes through crisis is by no means comfortable. It often means acknowledging painful truths about the person you loved, the relationship you invested in, and the precious time spent doing all of the above. It means facing the reality that the future you'd been hoping for was never going to materialize and that the life you've been living has been built on a foundation of lies.

But this clarity, however painful, is also liberating. It's the beginning of freedom. It's the first step toward reclaiming your life, your sanity, and your soul. It's the moment when you stop being a victim of circumstances and start becoming the author of your own story.

Discernment vs. Gaslighting: Reclaiming Your Inner Voice

One of the most cunning aspects of emotional terrorism is how it systematically undermines your ability to trust your own perceptions. The Cat has spent months or years convincing you that your intuition is paranoia, your concerns are overreactions, and your feelings are invalid. They've trained you to doubt your own mind and defer to their version of reality.

But your awakening is often marked by the return of your discernment, stronger and clearer than ever before. This is the voice that always knew something was wrong, even when you couldn't articulate what it was. This is the voice that tried to warn you about red flags you chose to ignore, or connections you knew weren't on the up-and-up. This is the voice that whispered truth when the Cat, flying monkeys, and the enablers (Chapter 8) were speaking lies.

Realize that discernment is not your enemy. It's not "messing things up" or the reason your relationship is struggling. Discernment is actually a great ally, your internal guidance system, your God-given ability to perceive truth beyond what your eyes can see or your ears can hear.

The Cat worked so hard to silence this voice because they knew it was a threat to their control over you. They knew that if you ever started trusting your own perceptions again, their house of cards would come tumbling down. They knew that your discernment would eventually expose their lies, reveal their manipulation, and guide you toward freedom.

Learning to trust yourself again takes practice. You've been trained to second-guess yourself, to seek external validation for your internal experiences, and to prioritize other people's comfort over the truth. But every time you cultivate and honor your discernment, you strengthen this crucial connection to your authentic self.

Discernment will tell you when someone's words don't match their actions. It will alert you to danger before your logical mind has processed all the evidence. It will guide you toward people and situations that honor your worth and away from those that diminish it. Let it become your compass as you navigate your way back to wholeness.

Breaking Through Denial

Denial is a powerful psychological defense mechanism that protects us from truths we're not ready to handle. In the context of emotional terrorism, denial serves as a buffer between your conscious mind and the devastating reality of your situation. It allows you to function day to day without being overwhelmed by the full scope of what you're enduring.

But, as we've discussed, denial also keeps you trapped. It prevents you from taking the actions necessary to protect yourself and change your circumstances. It allows abuse to continue unchecked because you're not fully acknowledging its existence or impact. It keeps you hoping for change that will never come.

Breaking through denial is often a gradual process, though it can sometimes happen in a sudden moment of clarity. It usually begins with small admissions of truth that you've been avoiding. Maybe you admit that their promises have been consistently broken. Maybe you finally acknowledge that their behavior is getting worse, not better.

This was the gradual awakening for me, as I began to systematically chart the mood swings, manic episodes, and aggressive arguments using one simple tool: a calendar. With years of data collected, organized, and analyzed, I had successfully clocked World War III to happen every three months, followed by the welcomed relief of a honeymoon phase with unfortunate accuracy.

These small cracks in your denial eventually become larger fissures, and larger fissures eventually become complete breaks. The wall of protection that denial provided comes crashing down, and you're left to face the full reality of your situation. This can be overwhelming, terrifying, and deeply painful.

But it's also the beginning of your liberation.

When you break through denial, you stop wasting energy on false hope and start investing it in real solutions. You stop trying to fix someone who doesn't want to be fixed and start focusing on healing yourself. Now you can stop waiting for them to change and start taking responsibility for changing your own circumstances.

Breaking through denial doesn't mean becoming cynical or losing your capacity for hope and love. It means becoming realistic about what is while maintaining faith in what could be. It means accepting the truth about your current situation while believing in your ability to create a different future.

Know that the process of breaking through denial is often accompanied by *grief*. You're mourning the loss of the relationship you thought you had, the future you thought you were building, and the person you thought you loved. This grief is real and valid, and it's an important part of your healing process.

So don't stifle it. Don't muffle it or try to rush it out the door. Feel all the feels that grieving brings and take as long as it takes.

Because on the other side of this grief is freedom. On the other side of denial is truth. And on the other side of truth is the possibility of a life that honors your worth, respects your dignity, and celebrates your authentic self.

Cat Tactics Decoded

The Awakening Sabotage: When the Cat senses that you're beginning to see the situation clearly—and they're not ready for the game to be over—they often escalate their manipulation tactics. They might become more charming, more apologetic, or more threatening. They might promise dramatic changes, threaten dire consequences, or create crises that demand your immediate attention. This is designed to pull you back into the fog of confusion before your total awakening can solidify into action.

The Reality Revision: The Cat will attempt to rewrite history, deny events that happened, minimize their impact, or claim that you're remembering things incorrectly. This is designed to make you doubt your own memories and perceptions.

The Isolation Intensification: As your awakening progresses, the Cat may try to cut you off from sources of support, validation, or alternative perspectives. They might criticize your friends, limit your access to family, or create conflicts that force you to choose between them and your support system. This tactic is especially popular with hypochondriacal Cats—the ones who consistently fake illnesses to manipulate your empathy and care. "So, you're just going to go out with your friends and leave me here alone like this?!" It was always amazing how often the Cat had panic attacks or needed an ambulance and full-blown medical attention when it was time for me to hang out with my friends. They know that isolation makes it eventually easier to control your emotions and your reality.

Mouse Traps

The Awakening Guilt: You feel guilty for finally seeing the truth about your situation because it means acknowledging that you've been living a lie. You might feel dumb for not seeing it sooner, angry at yourself for staying so long, or ashamed that you allowed yourself to be treated so poorly. This guilt can actually pull you back into denial because facing the truth feels too painful. Be careful with guilt— and keep going.

The Change Fantasy: Even after your awakening, you might still harbor hope that your new clarity will somehow inspire them to change. Some of you are smiling or laughing out loud because you know it's true—don't drink your own Kool-Aid. You might think that if you can just explain what you've realized, they'll have their *own* awakening, and the relationship can be saved. This fantasy can keep you engaged in trying to fix the unfixable instead of focusing on your own healing and freedom.

The Timing Trap: You convince yourself that now isn't the right time to act on your awakening. Maybe it's the holidays, or they're going through a difficult time, or they're having more frequent panic attacks, or you don't have enough money saved, or the children need stability. While practical considerations are important, this trap can keep you waiting indefinitely for the "perfect" time that will probably never come.

The Proof Paralysis: You feel like you need *more* evidence, *more* certainty, or *more* validation before you can trust your awakening. You might think you need to document more incidents on your calendar or in your diary, gather more support, or be absolutely certain before you take action. This can keep you stuck in *analysis mode* instead of taking action toward freedom.

Nurturing Your Awakening

Your awakening is precious and fragile. It needs to be protected, nurtured, and strengthened if it's going to survive the inevitable attempts to undermine it. The Cat will not accept your new clarity gracefully. They will fight to pull you back into the wilderness of confusion, doubt, and false hope.

Nurturing your awakening means surrounding yourself with people who validate your perceptions and support truth. It means limiting your exposure to those who gaslight you, minimize your experiences, or pressure you to "work things out." It means choosing to spend time with people who remind you of who you really are, rather than those who reinforce the distorted version of yourself that the Cat created.

Here are refresher steps you can take to nurture and protect your awakening:

1. **Document** your experiences so you can't be convinced that they didn't happen or weren't as bad as you remember. Write down your thoughts and feelings so you can track your progress and remind yourself of your truth when doubt creeps in. Create a record of your awakening that you can return to when the fog tries to roll back in.

2. **Educate** yourself about emotional abuse, narcissistic behavior, and trauma bonding so you can understand what you've experienced and why it's been so difficult to leave. Knowledge is power, and understanding the dynamics of your situation will help you make informed decisions about your future.

3. Most importantly, **trust yourself**. Believe your own experiences, honor your own feelings, and respect your own perceptions. Refuse to let anyone convince you that the truth of what you've experienced isn't valid or that your awakening is just another overreaction.

Your awakening is not a phase you'll grow out of. It's not a temporary emotional state that will pass if you just wait long enough. It's not a mistake or an overreaction or a sign that you're being too sensitive. Your awakening is your soul's way of guiding you back to abundant life, back to truth.

In the next chapter, we'll explore how to channel your awakening into action by building a practical escape plan. We'll discuss safety planning, resource gathering, and the concrete steps you can take to move from awareness to freedom, regardless of your current circumstances.

For now, honor your awakening. Trust truth. And remember that the same Tenacity that got you through this situation is more than enough to get you out of it.

IV

SECTION IV: RECLAIMING THE MOUSE'S IDENTITY

14

Chapter 14: The Tenacious Spirit: Building Your Escape Plan

"She is clothed with strength and dignity; she can laugh at the days to come." -
Proverbs 31:25

Your awakening was the moment you realized the truth. Now comes the moment you decide to *act* on it.

Building an escape plan isn't about admitting defeat. It's about acknowledging reality and taking responsibility for your own safety, sanity, and future. It's about channeling your intelligence, your courage, and your Tenacious spirit into creating a path toward freedom.

This isn't the romantic notion of escape you see on Lifetime or Netflix, where someone dramatically walks out the door with nothing but their dignity intact. Real escape from emotional terrorism requires strategy, preparation, and careful planning. It requires the same intelligence and determination that got you through everything else in your life, applied now to the most important project you'll ever undertake: *saving yourself.*

No two escape plans are identical. My escape plan may look different from yours, but the principles and strategies shared here still apply. While I escaped the grips of rejection and abandonment as the Cat exited the game for the New Year's Eve supply, you must have an escape plan to survive and move forward toward a brighter future.

So, whether you're planning to leave physically, emotionally, or both, whether your timeline is weeks, months, or years, whether your situation involves marriage, children, finances, or other complications, this chapter will help you build a plan that prioritizes your safety while honoring your unique circumstances.

Remember: you don't have to have all the answers right now. You don't have to have unlimited resources or perfect conditions. You just have to start where you are, with what you have, and take the next right step for you.

The Foundation: Safety First

Before we talk about logistics, resources, or timelines, we need to establish the most important principle of any escape plan: your safety comes first. Always. No exceptions.

Leaving an abusive relationship is often the most dangerous time for the victim. The Cat's need for control intensifies when they sense they're losing their grip on you. They may escalate their manipulation, threats, or even physical violence when they realize you're serious about leaving.

This doesn't mean you shouldn't leave. It means you need to leave smart.

Safety planning isn't just about physical safety, though that's certainly a crucial component. It's also about emotional safety, financial safety, legal safety, and social safety. It's about protecting yourself from retaliation, manipulation, and the various ways the Cat might try to punish you for choosing yourself over their control.

Physical Safety Considerations:

- Do you have a safe place to go if you need to leave immediately?
- Are there weapons in the home that could be used against you?
- Does the Cat have a history of physical violence or threats?
- Do you have a way to communicate with help if you're in immediate danger?

- Are there children whose safety also needs to be considered?

Emotional Safety Considerations:

- Do you have people in your life who support your decision and won't try to talk you out of it?
- Are you prepared for the emotional manipulation that will likely intensify when you start pulling away?
- Do you have coping strategies for the guilt, fear, and doubt that may arise?
- Are you ready for the smear campaign that may follow your departure?

Financial Safety Considerations:

- Do you have access to your own money or the ability to earn your own income?
- Are you aware of all joint assets, debts, and financial obligations?
- Do you have important financial documents or copies of them in a safe place?
- Are you prepared for potential financial retaliation or sabotage?

Legal Safety Considerations:

- Do you understand your legal rights regarding property, children, and financial support?
- Do you have documentation of abuse that might be relevant in legal proceedings?
- Are you aware of restraining order procedures if they become necessary?
- Do you have access to legal advice or representation?

Resource Gathering: Building Your Arsenal

Escaping emotional terrorism requires resources: financial, emotional, practical, and informational. Start gathering these resources now, even if you're not ready to use them yet. Think of this as building your arsenal for freedom.

Financial Resources: Money is often the biggest barrier to leaving an abusive relationship. The Cat may have deliberately created financial dependence to make it harder for you to leave. Start building your financial independence gradually and carefully:

- Open a bank account in your name only, preferably at a different bank than any joint accounts
- Start setting aside small amounts of cash whenever possible
- Research your earning potential and job opportunities in your field
- Understand your rights to marital assets and support
- Gather important financial documents (tax returns, bank statements, investment/401K accounts, insurance policies)
- Research assistance programs for domestic violence survivors
- Consider selling items you own individually to build a small emergency fund

Emotional Resources: Leaving an abusive relationship requires tremendous emotional strength. Start building your emotional reserves now:

- Reconnect with supportive friends and family members
- Consider working with a therapist who understands narcissistic abuse
- Join support groups for abuse survivors (online or in person)
- Read books and articles about narcissistic abuse and recovery
- Practice self-care activities that restore your emotional energy
- Develop coping strategies for stress, anxiety, and depression
- Build a network of people who validate your experiences and support your healing

Practical Resources: Freedom requires practical preparation. Start gathering the tools and information you'll need:

- Secure copies of important documents (birth certificates, passports, social security cards, marriage certificate, medical records)
- Research housing options (temporary and long-term)
- Investigate childcare options if you have children
- Research legal aid services and domestic violence resources in your area
- Prepare a "go bag" with essential items in case you need to leave quickly
- Research transportation options and ensure you have access to a vehicle or other means of travel
- Update your resume and professional references

Informational Resources: Knowledge is power. The more you understand about your situation, your rights, and your options, the better equipped you'll be to make informed decisions:

- Learn about narcissistic abuse and trauma bonding
- Research your legal rights regarding divorce, child custody, and property division
- Understand the resources available to domestic violence survivors in your area
- Learn about safety planning and protective measures
- Research the warning signs of escalating abuse
- Understand the tactics abusers use to maintain control during separation

Building Your Support Network

One of the most crucial aspects of your escape plan is building a network of people who understand your situation and support your decision to prioritize your safety and well-being. This network will be your lifeline during the difficult process of leaving and rebuilding your life.

Identifying True Allies: Not everyone in your current social circle will be supportive of your decision to leave—especially those you've already identified as flying monkeys or enablers. Some people may try to talk you out of it, minimize your experiences, or pressure you to "work things out." You need to identify who your true allies are before you need them.

True allies are people who:

- Believe your experiences without requiring proof and hard receipts
- Support your right to prioritize your own safety and happiness
- Respect your decisions even if they don't fully understand them
- Offer practical help without judgment or conditions
- Maintain confidentiality when you ask them to
- Don't try to fix your relationship or convince you to stay
- Don't play both sides and tell the Cat about your decision and plans

Professional Support: Consider building relationships with professionals who can provide specialized help:

- Therapists who specialize in narcissistic abuse and trauma
- Legal professionals who understand domestic violence cases
- Financial advisors who can help you understand your options
- Domestic violence advocates who can guide you through available resources
- Medical professionals who can document any physical or mental effects of abuse

Peer Support: Connecting with other survivors can provide some validation, encouragement, and practical advice from people who truly understand what you're going through:

- Online support groups for narcissistic abuse survivors
- Local domestic violence support groups
- Therapy groups for abuse survivors
- Informal networks of friends who've been through similar experiences

Creating Backup Plans: Your support network should include people who can help in different ways and at different times:

- Someone who can provide emergency housing if you need to leave quickly
- Someone who can help with childcare during the transition
- Someone who can provide transportation if needed
- Someone who can help with legal or financial matters
- Someone who can provide emotional support during difficult moments

Documentation Strategies

Documentation serves multiple purposes in your escape plan. It helps you remember the reality of your situation when gaslighting makes you doubt yourself. It provides evidence if legal proceedings become necessary. And it helps you track patterns of behavior that might be important for your safety planning.

What to Document:

- Incidents of verbal, emotional, or physical abuse (dates, times, details, witnesses)
- Threats made against you, your children, or your property
- Attempts to isolate you from friends, family, or support systems
- Financial abuse or control tactics
- Violations of boundaries or agreements
- Evidence of substance abuse or other concerning behaviors
- Communications that demonstrate manipulation or abuse (texts, emails, voicemails)

How to Document Safely:

- Use a private email account that the Cat doesn't have access to
- Store documentation in a secure location outside your home
- Consider using a trusted friend's address for sensitive mail

- Take photos of any physical evidence (injuries, damaged property, threatening notes)
- Keep a journal in a secure location or online account
- Save screenshots of abusive texts or social media posts
- Consider using apps designed for privately documenting domestic violence, e.g., TapeACall or VictimsVoice.

Legal Considerations:

- Understand the laws in your state regarding recording conversations; "one-party" consent states generally allow you to record conversations in which you are a party (and thus giving the single required consent). Consult your legal professional.
- Know what types of evidence are admissible in court
- Consider having documentation reviewed by a legal professional
- Understand how documentation might be used in custody proceedings
- Be aware of privacy laws and the Cat's rights regarding certain types of evidence

Creating Your Timeline

Your escape plan needs a timeline, but it also needs flexibility. Circumstances can change quickly in abusive relationships, and you need to be prepared to accelerate your timeline if your safety is at risk.

Immediate Safety Plan (0-30 days):

- Identify safe places you can go in an emergency
- Prepare a "go bag" with essential items
- Establish code words with trusted friends or family
- Memorize important phone numbers
- Identify the safest times to leave if necessary
- Plan how to protect children if they're involved

- Research immediate resources (shelters, hotlines, emergency services)

Short-term Plan (1-6 months):

- Build financial resources and independence
- Strengthen your support network
- Gather important documents and evidence
- Research housing and employment options
- Begin legal consultations if necessary
- Start therapy or counseling
- Develop coping strategies for the transition period

Long-term Plan (6 months and beyond):

- Establish financial independence
- Secure stable housing
- Finalize legal proceedings if necessary
- Focus on healing and recovery
- Rebuild your social network
- Pursue personal and professional goals
- Create a life that reflects your values and priorities

Cat Tactics Decoded

The Escalation Response: When the Cat senses you're pulling away or making plans to leave, they often escalate their behavior. This might include increased surveillance, threats of self-harm, or promises of dramatic change. This escalation is designed to either scare you into staying or convince you that leaving isn't necessary.

The Resource Sabotage: The Cat may try to sabotage your ability to gather resources by monitoring your finances, limiting your access to money, interfering with your employment, or damaging your credit. They understand that financial dependence is one of the strongest chains keeping you in bondage.

The False Emergency: The Cat may create or exaggerate crises that require your immediate attention and presence. These "emergencies" often coincide with times when you're making progress on your escape plan or spending time away from them. This tactic is designed to keep you focused on their needs rather than your own plans.

The Blackmail Campaign: If your experience resembles mine, the Cat will fire off threats of blackmail and smear campaigns to make you rethink your plans to leave. This is when the Cat threatens to expose secrets and intimate details they learned about you in the relationship: your trauma wounds, history of abuse, family secrets, intimacy details, financial status—nothing will be off limits or beneath the fruit of their hatred. This tactic is designed to emotionally terrorize your past so you can't focus on your better future.

Mouse Traps

The Perfect Plan Trap: You convince yourself that you need to have every detail figured out to a tee before you can take any action. While planning is important, waiting for the perfect plan can keep you trapped indefinitely. Sometimes you have to start moving before the whole path materializes.

The Guilt Trap: You feel guilty for "abandoning" someone who "needs" you, especially if they're going through a difficult time or making promises to change. Remember that you're not required to sacrifice your well-being for theirs, and staying in an abusive situation doesn't actually help them grow or heal, either.

The Children Trap: You convince yourself that staying is better for the children, even though research consistently shows that children are harmed by witnessing domestic violence and emotional abuse. Protecting yourself *is* actually protecting your children.

The Financial Fear Trap: You believe you can't survive financially on your own, so you stay in a situation that's destroying your mental and emotional health. While financial concerns are valid, there are resources available to help you transition to independence, and your wellness is worth it.

Moving from Planning to Action

Having a plan is crucial, but at some point, you have to move from planning to action. This transition can be terrifying, especially when you've been conditioned to doubt your own judgment and fear the consequences of asserting your independence.

Remember that taking action doesn't necessarily mean making dramatic, irreversible changes overnight. It might mean taking small actions that build momentum and confidence. Each step forward proves to yourself that you're capable of creating change in your life. Each move toward independence weakens the Cat's control over you.

Your Tenacious spirit is what got you through everything you've endured so far. That same spirit will carry you through the process of building and executing your escape plan. Trust yourself. Trust your strength. Trust your ability to create a better life. Trust God.

In the next chapter, we'll explore how to establish and maintain healthy boundaries as you begin to reclaim and execute your power. These boundaries will become your new defense system, protecting you from future manipulation and abuse while you heal and rebuild your life.

For now, remember that planning your escape isn't giving up on love. It's refusing to accept a counterfeit version of love that destroys rather than nurtures your soul.

15

Chapter 15: The High-Value Woman's Recovery Timeline

"He heals the brokenhearted and binds up their wounds." – Psalm 147:3 NIV

Sis, let's get something straight right from the start: there is no such thing as a perfect healing and recovery timeline. There's no magic formula that says you should be "over it" in six months, feeling better in a year, or completely healed in two years. Anyone who tries to put your healing on a deadline doesn't understand the first thing about what you've been through.

Recovery from emotional terrorism or narcissistic abuse isn't like recovering from a broken bone, where you can predict that in six to eight weeks you'll be back to normal. It's more like recovering from a complex injury that affects multiple systems in your body simultaneously. Some days you'll feel like you're making incredible progress. Other days you'll feel like you're back at square one. Both experiences are completely normal and part of the process.

The timeline example I'm about to share with you isn't a prescription. It's not an orderly checklist wrapped in a neat bow that you need to complete. It's simply a map with hypothetical timestamps that shows you the general territory of healing, with the understanding that your journey will be uniquely yours. You might spend longer in some phases and breeze through others. You might circle back to earlier phases when you thought you were done with them. You might experience multiple phases at the same darn time. Whew!

What matters isn't how fast you heal or how perfectly you navigate each phase. The goal is not to get a 100% on the test. What matters is that you keep moving forward, even when forward feels like sideways, upside down, or sometimes even backward.

Understanding the Landscape of Healing

Before we dive into the specific phases, you need to understand something crucial about trauma recovery: it's not linear. Honey, you will not find a Beautiful, straight line from broken to healed, from victim to survivor, from wounded to whole. It's more like a spiral staircase hanging off a few bolts, where you revisit similar themes and challenges at deeper levels as you grow stronger and more capable of handling them.

This non-linear nature of healing can be incredibly frustrating, especially for high-achieving women who are used to setting goals, making plans, and seeing measurable progress. You might feel like you're failing when you have a bad day after a string of good ones, or like you're weak when an old trigger catches you off guard months into your recovery.

Here's what I need you to understand: setbacks aren't failures. Yeah, we hate that word, but you're not failing—it's all part of the recovery process. Healing happens in waves that ebb and flow. Sometimes you need to take two steps back to gather the strength for three steps ahead of you. Sometimes you need to revisit an old wound with new wisdom before you can truly release it.

Your recovery timeline is not a reflection of your worth, your strength, or your commitment to healing. It's simply the unique path your soul needs to take to find its way back to freedom and wholeness.

Phase One: Crisis and Survival (Months 0-6)

This is where most women find themselves when they first realize they've been living in an abusive situation. You might be in this phase right now, reading these words while your world feels like it's falling apart around you.

If so, I want you to know that what you're experiencing is normal, necessary, and best of all—temporary.

What This Phase Looks Like: The crisis phase is characterized by emotional chaos, physical symptoms, and a complete disruption of your normal coping mechanisms. You might feel like you're losing your mind, like nothing makes sense anymore, like the person you used to be has disappeared entirely.

You might experience:

- Intense emotional swings from rage to despair to depressed numbness
- Physical symptoms like insomnia, constant sleep, loss of appetite, or deep fatigue
- Difficulty concentrating or making even simple decisions
- Intrusive thoughts about the abuse or the abuser
- Hyper-vigilance or feeling constantly on edge
- Social withdrawal or desperate clinging to others
- Questioning everything you thought you knew about love, relationships, and yourself

Your Primary Goals: During this phase, your only job is survival. You're not trying to heal completely or figure out your entire future. As fabulous as you are, don't even try to help someone else with their oxygen mask—because it diverts your attention from the situation you're in. Simply try to get through each moment, minute, hour, day, and week with your sanity and safety intact.

Focus on:

- Establishing basic safety (physical, emotional, financial)
- Meeting your fundamental needs (food, sleep, shelter, medical care)
- Building or rebuilding a support system
- Limiting as much contact as possible with the abuser
- Avoiding major life decisions when possible
- Being incredibly gentle with yourself
- Practicing basic self-care, e.g., bathing, brushing your teeth, doing your hair—breathing!

What Healing Looks Like Here: Progress in this phase might look like having one good hour in a terrible day, sleeping through the night once a week, or reaching out to a friend when you're struggling. One of my wins was eating at least two meals a day after grief had snatched my appetite. These might seem like minuscule victories, but they're actually enormous accomplishments given what you're dealing with.

Don't expect to feel better quickly. Don't expect to have clarity about your future. Don't expect to be the strong, capable woman you used to be. Right now, you're in triage mode, and that's exactly where you need to be.

Phase Two: Stabilization and Understanding (Months 6-18)

As the initial crisis begins to settle, you focus on creating stability and begin to understand what happened to you. This is when you start to make sense of the chaos and develop the tools you'll need for deeper healing.

What This Phase Looks Like: The emotional roller coaster begins to level out somewhat, though you may still have difficult days. You start to develop routines and coping strategies that help you feel more grounded. You begin to educate yourself about abuse, trauma, and recovery.

You might experience:

· More stable emotions with occasional intense episodes
· Improved sleep and appetite, though still not completely normal
· Increased ability to concentrate and make decisions
· Growing awareness of how the abuse affected you
· Anger at the abuser and possibly at yourself
· Grief for what you lost and what you never had
· Cautious hope about the future

Your Primary Goals: This phase is about building the foundation for deeper healing. You're creating stability in your daily life while beginning to process what happened to you.

Focus on:

- Establishing consistent routines and self-care practices
- Learning about trauma, abuse, and recovery
- Working with a therapist who understands narcissistic abuse
- Rebuilding your support network
- Setting and maintaining boundaries
- Processing the relationship and its impact on you
- Beginning to repossess your identity

What Healing Looks Like Here: Progress might look like going five days or more without crying, having the energy to cook a real meal, or setting a boundary and sticking to it. For me, it was having a conversation about something other than the trauma or what the Cat did, as the shock from impact began to wear off. Know that you're building the skills and stability you'll need for the deeper work ahead.

Phase Three: Processing and Integration (Months 18-36)

This is often the most challenging phase of recovery because it's when you do the deep work of processing your trauma and integrating the lessons learned into your new sense of self. The crisis has passed, you've stabilized, and now you're ready to really dig into the healing work.

What This Phase Looks Like: You have more emotional capacity to handle difficult feelings and memories. You're able to look at the relationship and its impact on you with more clarity and less reactivity, though a stray trigger may catch you off guard with lighter impact. You begin to see patterns and make connections between your past and present.

You might experience:

- Waves of grief as you fully process what you lost
- Anger that feels safer to express and explore
- Memories or realizations that you weren't ready to handle before
- A stronger sense of your own identity and values
- Increased confidence in your ability to handle challenges

- Moments of genuine joy, gratitude, and hope for the future
- Occasional setbacks that feel less devastating

Your Primary Goals: This phase is about doing the deep work of healing while continuing to build the life you want to live.

Focus on:

- Processing trauma through therapy, journaling, or other healing modalities
- Exploring how the abuse affected your beliefs about yourself and relationships
- Developing a stronger sense of your authentic self
- Learning to trust your own perceptions and judgment
- Building healthy relationships and letting go of toxic ones
- Pursuing goals and interests that were neglected
- Developing a vision for your future

What Healing Looks Like Here: Progress might look like being able to tell your story without falling apart, standing up for yourself in a difficult situation, pursuing a goal you'd given up on, or feeling genuinely happy for an entire day. I remember thinking, "how in the world am I still here?" You're not just surviving anymore; you're beginning to thrive.

Phase Four: Rebuilding and Growth (Months 36+)

This phase is about applying everything you've learned to build a life that reflects your true values, desires, and potential. You're not just healing from what happened to you; you're creating something Beautiful from the ashes.

What This Phase Looks Like: You have a solid sense of who you are and what you want from life. You've processed the major trauma and developed healthy coping skills. You're able to have healthy relationships and pursue meaningful goals.

You might experience:

- A strong sense of your own identity and worth
- Confidence in your ability to handle whatever life throws at you
- Healthy relationships based on mutual respect and genuine connection
- Joy and fulfillment in your daily life
- Occasional triggers or difficult days that you can handle with your new coping skills
- A sense of purpose and meaning that may have grown from your experience
- The ability to help others who are going through similar struggles

Your Primary Goals: This phase is about living fully and authentically while maintaining the healing you've achieved.
Focus on:

- Building and maintaining healthy relationships
- Pursuing your goals and dreams with confidence
- Continuing to practice self-care and boundary-setting
- Using your experience to help others when appropriate
- Staying connected to your support system
- Continuing to grow and evolve as a person
- Celebrating how far you've come

What Healing Looks Like Here: Progress might look like falling in love again (with yourself first, then someone else), achieving a goal you thought was impossible, helping another woman escape abuse, or simply waking up most days feeling grateful for your life. You're not just surviving or even healing; you're thriving.

The Grief Process: Your Constant Companion

Throughout all phases of recovery, grief can be your constant companion. You're not just grieving the end of a relationship; you're grieving multiple losses that occurred over an extended period of time.

What You're Grieving:

- The person you thought your abuser was
- The relationship you thought you had
- The future you thought you were building together
- The time you lost to the abuse
- The person you were before the abuse
- Your innocence and trust
- Your sense of safety in the world
- The support of people who didn't believe you
- The dreams you gave up or put on hold

The Stages of Grief (Not Linear):

- **Denial**: "It wasn't that bad." "They didn't mean it." "I'm overreacting."
- **Anger**: At them, at yourself, at others who didn't help, at the unfairness of it all
- **Bargaining**: "If only I had..." "Maybe if I try..." "What if I..."
- **Depression**: The deep sadness of fully accepting what you've lost
- **Acceptance**: Not that what happened was okay, but that it happened and you're going to be okay anyway

Remember that grief doesn't follow a schedule. You might cycle through these stages multiple times, experience several simultaneously, or skip some entirely. There's no right or wrong way to grieve, and there's no timeline for when you should be "over it."

Managing Setbacks Like a High-Value Woman

Again, setbacks are not failures. They're information. They tell you what you still need to work on, what triggers you haven't fully processed, or what situations you're not quite ready to handle yet. A high-value woman doesn't see setbacks as evidence of her inadequacy; she sees them as data for her continued growth.

When You Have a Bad Day:

- Remember that one bad day doesn't erase weeks or months of progress
- Use your coping skills instead of abandoning them
- Reach out to your support system
- Be as gentle with yourself as you would be with a good friend or your child
- Look for the lesson or information the setback is providing
- Recommit to your healing without judgment

When You Feel Like You're Going Backward:

- Remember that healing happens in spirals, not straight lines
- Consider whether you're processing something at a deeper level
- Check whether you're taking on too much or neglecting self-care
- Evaluate whether you need additional support or resources
- Trust that this difficult period will pass, just like the others have

When Others Question Your Progress:

- Remember that your healing timeline belongs to you alone—no one gets a vote
- Don't let the impatience of others rush your process
- Surround yourself with people who understand trauma recovery
- Trust your own assessment of your progress over others' opinions

Cat Tactics Decoded

The Recovery Sabotage: If the Cat is still in your life in any capacity, they may try to sabotage your healing by creating crises during your stable periods, love-bombing you when you're making progress, or spreading lies about your mental health to others. They understand that your recovery threatens their control over you.

The False Timeline: The Cat may try to rush your healing by demanding forgiveness, reconciliation, or "moving on" before you're ready. They might claim that your continued healing work is evidence that you're "stuck in the past", "refusing to forgive", or "choosing to be a victim." This is manipulation designed to stop your progress.

The Healing Hijack: The Cat might try to insert themselves into your healing process by claiming they're also working on themselves, demanding to be part of your therapy, or using your recovery language to manipulate you. "I'm being gentle with my mistakes, and forgiving myself, too." They may present themselves as a fellow victim or claim they've changed based on your healing work.

Mouse Traps

The Comparison Trap: You compare your healing timeline to others' and feel like you're falling behind or taking too long. Remember that everyone's healing journey is different, and comparing your internal experience to someone else's external experience is never accurate or helpful.

The Perfection Trap: You expect your healing to be smooth and linear, and you judge yourself harshly for setbacks or difficult days. Healing is messy, non-linear, and full of ups and downs. Perfection is not the goal; progress is.

The Rush Trap: You try to speed up your healing because you're tired of dealing with the pain or because others are pressuring you to "move on." Healing won't be rushed, and trying to skip steps often means you'll have to revisit them later. Trust me, there are no CliffNotes to healing from emotional terrorism.

The Plateau Trap: You mistake a stable period for the end of your healing journey and stop doing the work that got you there. Mountain top experiences are amazing, and you'll want to stay there forever, but your journey will involve some valley terrain. Don't be afraid, the valley experiences will pass, too. Healing is an ongoing process, not a destination you reach and then abandon.

Your Unique Timeline

Your recovery timeline will be influenced by many factors: the length and severity of the abuse, your support system, your access to resources, your previous trauma history, your natural resilience and tenacity, and countless other variables. Some women heal faster; others take longer. Neither is better or worse.

What matters is that you *honor* your own process, trust your own timeline, and refuse to let anyone else dictate how fast you should heal or what your recovery should look like. You are not a machine that can be repaired on a schedule. You are a human being with a complex inner world that deserves time, patience, and compassion to heal.

Your healing is not a race. It's not a competition. It's not a performance for others to judge. Don't weaponize your High-Value against yourself. Healing is a sacred journey back to yourself, and it will take exactly as long as it takes.

In the next chapter, we'll explore one of the most Courageous things you'll ever do—set and keep healthy boundaries.

For now, remember: you are exactly where you need to be in your healing journey, even if it doesn't feel like it's enough.

16

Chapter 16: Courageous Boundaries: Your New Defense System

"Above all else, guard your heart, for everything you do flows from it." - Proverbs 4:23

If you've never had healthy boundaries before, the concept might feel foreign, selfish, or even cruel. You might have been taught that boundaries are walls that keep love out, barriers that prevent intimacy, or evidence of an unforgiving heart. You might believe that truly loving someone means having no limits, no conditions, and no protection for yourself.

Those are some of the most dangerous lies ever told.

Boundaries aren't walls that keep love out. They're gates that keep harm out while allowing real love to flow freely. They aren't barriers to intimacy. They're the foundation that makes genuine intimacy possible. Boundaries aren't evidence of an unforgiving heart. They're proof of a wise, discerning heart that has learned to protect what is precious.

After surviving emotional terrorism, boundaries aren't just helpful. They're essential. They're your new defense system, your early warning detection mechanism, and your protection plan all rolled into one. They're how you ensure that you never accept another invitation to a cat-and-mouse game of abuse.

Learning to set and maintain healthy boundaries is one of the most Courageous things you'll ever do in any relationship dynamic. It requires you to know and value yourself enough to protect yourself, to trust your own judgment enough to act on it, and to love yourself enough to disappoint people who don't understand your heart's protection plan.

Understanding the Boundary Spectrum

Boundaries exist on a spectrum from completely open to completely closed, and healthy people move fluidly along this spectrum depending on the situation, the relationship, and their own needs and capacity. The goal isn't to have the same boundaries with everyone. The goal is to have appropriate boundaries that match the level of trust, safety, and intimacy in each relationship.

Healthy Boundaries are flexible, appropriate to the situation, and based on your values, needs, and safety. They allow for connection while protecting your well-being. They can be adjusted as relationships grow and change, but they're not negotiable when it comes to your fundamental rights and dignity.

Rigid Boundaries are inflexible walls that keep everyone at a distance. While these might be necessary for a time during healing, they're not sustainable long-term because they prevent the connection and intimacy that humans need to thrive.

Porous Boundaries are so flexible that they offer no real protection. People with porous boundaries often struggle to say no, take on other people's emotions as their own, and allow others to violate their space, time, and energy without consequence.

Absent Boundaries mean there's no protection at all. People with absent boundaries often don't recognize when they're being violated; they've never exercised their right to set limits on how others treat them.

The Cat in your life likely exploited porous or absent boundaries, gradually training you to accept less and less respect while giving more and more of yourself. They convinced you that having boundaries was selfish, that protecting yourself was cruel, and that true love meant unlimited, unconditional access to your time, energy, and resources.

Now you're learning a different truth: boundaries are how you love yourself and others well.

Four Types of Boundaries

Understanding the different types of boundaries helps you identify where you need stronger protection and how to communicate your limits clearly:

Physical Boundaries

Physical boundaries protect your body, your personal space, and your physical environment. These include:

- Who can touch you, how, and when
- How much physical space you need to feel comfortable
- Who has access to your home and personal belongings
- Your right to physical safety and freedom from harm
- Your need for rest, nutrition, and medical care

Physical boundaries might sound like:

- "I'm not comfortable with hugging right now."
- "Please don't go through my personal belongings."
- "I need some space to think about this."
- "I won't tolerate being grabbed or pushed."

Emotional Boundaries

Emotional boundaries protect your feelings, your mental health, and your emotional energy. These include:

- What topics you're willing to discuss and when

- How much emotional support you can provide to others
- Your right to your own feelings without having them analyzed, dismissed, or minimized
- Protection from emotional manipulation and abuse
- Your need for emotional safety and validation

Emotional boundaries might sound like:

- "I'm not ready to talk about that yet."
- "I don't have the capacity to fix your problem right now."
- "My feelings are valid even if you don't understand them."
- "I won't accept being yelled at or called names."

Mental Boundaries

Mental boundaries protect your thoughts, beliefs, values, and decision-making autonomy. These include:

- Your right to your own opinions and beliefs
- Your ability to make decisions about your own life
- Protection from gaslighting and reality distortion
- Your intellectual autonomy and critical thinking
- Your right to change your mind

Mental boundaries might sound like:

- "I have a different perspective on this."
- "I'm not interested in your opinion of me."
- "I see what you're doing. I trust my own memory of what happened."
- "I won't be told what to think or believe. I don't have to validate my feelings."

Time and Energy Boundaries

Time and energy boundaries protect your most precious resources: your time, attention, and energy. These include:

- How you spend your time and with whom
- What activities and commitments you take on
- Your right to rest and recharge
- Protection from energy vampires and time wasters
- Your ability to prioritize your own needs and goals

Time and energy boundaries might sound like:

- "I'm not available for that right now."
- "I need to limit our conversations to 30 minutes."
- "I can't take on any additional commitments this month."
- "I need some time to myself to recharge."
- "That's not my responsibility or burden."

The Art of Boundary Communication

Setting boundaries isn't just about knowing what your limits are. It's about *communicating* them clearly, consistently, and without apology. This can feel terrifying at first, especially if you've been conditioned to believe that your needs don't matter or that setting limits makes you a bad person.

Be Clear and Specific. Vague boundaries are ineffective boundaries. Instead of saying "I need more respect," say "I won't continue this conversation if you raise your voice or call me names." Instead of "I need space," say "I need three days without contact to process what happened."

Use "I" Statements. Frame your boundaries in terms of what you will and won't do, not what the other person should or shouldn't do. This keeps the focus on your choices and removes the element of trying to control someone else's behavior.

Don't be J.A.D.E.D. You don't need to *justify, argue, defend, or over-explain* your boundaries or convince someone that they're reasonable. A simple, clear statement is enough: "I'm not comfortable with that" or "That doesn't work for me" is all it takes.

Stay Calm and Confident. Boundaries are not requests or suggestions. You're not asking permission to put a boundary here. They're statements of fact about how you will protect yourself. Deliver them with the same calm confidence you'd use to state any other fact.

Expect Push Back. People who have benefited from your lack of boundaries will not celebrate your newfound ability to protect yourself. They may argue, guilt-trip, manipulate, or escalate their behavior to try to get you to back down. This push back is actually confirmation that your boundary was necessary.

Enforcing Consequences

A boundary without a consequence *is* just a suggestion. If you're not prepared to follow through on your stated limits, you're not actually setting boundaries. You're making requests that others can choose to ignore.

Natural Consequences. Sometimes the consequence of violating your boundary is built into the boundary itself. If someone continues to yell at you after you've said you won't tolerate being yelled at, the natural consequence is that you leave the conversation or the room.

Logical Consequences. Logical consequences are directly related to the boundary violation. If someone repeatedly shows up at your home uninvited after you've asked them not to, the logical consequence might be that you don't answer the door or that you call the police.

Escalating Consequences. For repeated violations, consequences should escalate. The first violation might result in a conversation. The second might result in limited contact. The third might result in no contact for a specified period.

Following Through. The most important part of consequences is following through consistently. I often failed miserably with holding fast to my follow-through, and lost ground with my credibility in the process—but I didn't abort the mission. Just know that if you threaten a consequence but don't implement it, you've now taught the other person that your boundaries are negotiable and your words don't mean what they say.

Anticipating Boundary Violations

People who are used to having unlimited access to you will not accept your new boundaries gracefully. They will test them, push against them, and try to convince you to abandon them. Anticipating these tactics helps you stay strong when the pressure mounts.

The Guilt Trip. "I can't believe you're being so selfish." "After everything I've done for you." "You're hurting me by setting these limits." Remember: you are not responsible for managing other people's emotions about your boundaries.

The Minimization. "You're overreacting." "It's not that big of a deal." "You're being too sensitive." Your boundaries are valid regardless of whether others think they're necessary or reasonable.

The Negotiation. "Can't we compromise?" "Just this once?" "What if I promise to..." Boundaries are not starting points for negotiation. They're non-negotiable limits on what you will and won't accept.

The Escalation. When other tactics fail, some people will escalate their behavior to try to force you to back down. They might become more aggressive, more manipulative, or more desperate. This escalation is often a sign that your boundary is working and they're losing control.

The False Compliance. Some people will *appear* to accept your boundary while secretly planning to violate it later. They might agree to your limits in the moment, but then "forget" or claim they "misunderstood" them when they cross the line yet again.

Cat Tactics Decoded

The Boundary Erosion: The Cat will systematically test and push against your boundaries, starting with small violations to see if you'll enforce your limits. If you let small violations slide, they'll gradually increase in severity until your boundaries have completely vanished.

The Emergency Exception: The Cat will create or exaggerate crises that "require" you to temporarily suspend your boundaries. These emergencies often coincide with times when you're being consistent about your limits, and they're designed to make you feel guilty for maintaining your protection.

The Relationship Hostage: The Cat will threaten to end the relationship, withdraw their love, or punish you in other ways if you don't abandon your boundaries. This tactic exploits your fear of abandonment and your desire to preserve the relationship at any cost.

The Boundary Reversal: The Cat will claim that your boundaries are actually violations of their boundaries. This is a good one. They'll position your self-protection as aggression against them, making them the victim and you the bad guy for refusing to understand how unacceptable your treatment is to them.

Mouse Traps

The Guilt Trap: You feel guilty for setting boundaries because you've been conditioned to believe that protecting yourself is selfish. Remember that boundaries are actually loving because they create the conditions for healthy relationships to flourish.

The Perfection Trap: You believe you need to set perfect boundaries from the beginning and maintain them flawlessly. Boundary-setting is a skill that improves over time and with practice. It's okay to adjust, refine, and strengthen your boundaries as you learn.

The Explanation Trap: You feel like you need to justify your boundaries or convince others that they're reasonable. Your boundaries don't require a slide deck or anyone else's approval or understanding to be valid.

The Consistency Trap: You believe that if you can't maintain a boundary 100% of the time, there's no point in setting it at all. Even imperfectly maintained boundaries provide more protection than no boundaries at all.

Building Your Boundary Muscle

Like any skill, boundary-setting gets easier with practice. Start small and build your confidence before tackling the bigger, scarier boundaries you need to set.

Practice with Low-Stakes Situations. Start setting boundaries in situations where the consequences of pushback are minimal. Practice saying no to small requests, setting limits on your time with acquaintances, or protecting your energy in casual interactions.

Use Your Support System. Practice boundary conversations with trusted friends or family members before having them with more challenging people. Role-play difficult scenarios and get feedback on your communication style.

Document Your Boundaries. Write down your boundaries so you can refer to them when you're feeling pressured to abandon them. Having them in writing helps you stay consistent and reminds you why they're important.

Learn from Violations. When someone violates your boundary, use it as information. What does this tell you about this person's respect for you? What consequences do you need to implement? How can you strengthen this boundary going forward?

Celebrate Your Successes. Acknowledge and celebrate every time you successfully set or maintain a boundary, no matter how small. Each success builds your confidence and strengthens your boundary muscle.

The Freedom of Boundaries

Here's what might surprise you about boundaries: they don't limit your freedom. They create it. When you know what you will and won't accept, when you're clear about your limits and confident in your ability to enforce them, you can move through the world with a sense of safety and empowerment you've never experienced before.

Boundaries allow you to:

- Engage in relationships without fear of being taken advantage of (again)
- Give generously without depleting yourself
- Love others without losing yourself
- Trust your own judgment about people and situations
- Create space for the relationships and activities that truly matter to you

The people who respect your boundaries are the people who deserve access to your life. The people who consistently violate your boundaries are showing you exactly how much they value your well-being compared to their own desires.

Your boundaries are not suggestions. They're not starting points for negotiation. They're not evidence of your lack of love or forgiveness. They're statements of your worth, declarations of your dignity, and proof that you've learned to love yourself well.

In the next chapter, we'll explore how to declare 'Game Over' to the Cat-and-mouse dynamic once and for all. You'll learn how to step into your identity as a High-value, high-scoring woman who has not only survived emotional terrorism with flying colors, but has transformed it into unshakable wisdom and strength. It's time to officially end the game and walk away with your head held high.

For now, remember: you have the right to protect yourself, and protecting yourself is one of the most loving things you can do to make your heart happy.

V

SECTION V: GAME OVER - THIS IS YOUR NEW LIFE

17

Chapter 17: High-Value, High-Score: "Game Over"

"The end of a matter is better than its beginning; likewise, patience is better than pride." - Ecclesiastes 7:8 NIV

The game is over.

Not because you've reached some arbitrary finish line or achieved perfect healing. Not because you've confronted your abuser with a dramatic speech or received the apology you deserved. Not because you've proven your worth to anyone else, or checked every box from an e-book, course, or podcast recovery checklist.

Honey, the game is over because you say it is.

You learned the rules of the Cat-and-mouse dynamic. You're clear on the tactics, recognized the patterns, and can see through the illusions. You're healing your wounds, reclaiming your power, and rebuilding your life. You've discovered your worth, embraced your strength, and stepped into your purpose.

But most importantly, you've realized that you were never actually a Mouse at all. You were always a Woman—a High-value, high-scoring woman who temporarily forgot her own power.

The Cat didn't create your worth, and the Cat cannot destroy it. Your value was never up for debate, never dependent on someone else's treatment of you, never contingent on your performance in their twisted game.

This chapter isn't about what you need to do to end the game. It's about recognizing that you already have.

It's about declaring victory not because you've defeated the Cat or got your revenge, but because you've remembered who you are underneath all the lies and manipulation. You've re-membered the broken woman who now understands you were "fearfully and wonderfully made". It's about walking away with your head held high, not because you've won some competition, but because you've reclaimed first place in your life.

The game is over, and you get to decide what comes next.

The Power of Quiet Closure

When most people think about ending an abusive relationship or breaking free from emotional terrorism, they imagine dramatic confrontations, explosive arguments, or climactic moments of truth. They picture the victim finally standing up to the abuser, delivering a powerful speech about their worth, and walking away in triumph while the Cat realizes the error of their ways.

Confronting emotional terrorism is not a Hollywood production, and real liberation rarely looks like a movie scene.

Real liberation is often quiet. It's the moment you stop explaining yourself to someone who has no intention of understanding. It's the day you realize you don't need their permission to leave, their acknowledgment of the abuse to validate your experience, or another insincere apology to find peace. It's the gradual shift from asking "How do I make them understand?" to "How do I protect my peace?"

Before power can be reclaimed, it must first be recognized. This is what the power of quiet closure looks like:

No contact as a complete sentence. You don't owe anyone an explanation for protecting yourself. Blocking numbers, avoiding places, and refusing to engage isn't cruel - it's self-preservation. Your silence isn't punishment; it's peace.

Internal declarations matter more than external ones. The most important "game over" declaration happens in your own heart and mind. When you internally decide that you're done, that you deserve better, and that you're moving forward regardless of their perspective or response, the game truly ends.

Closure is a decision, not an event. You don't need a final conversation, a last meeting, or a formal goodbye to have closure. Closure happens when you decide to close the door on that chapter of your life and turn your attention to what's next.

Your healing doesn't require their participation. Your healing is not a group project. They don't need to acknowledge the harm they caused, take responsibility for their actions, beg your forgiveness, or validate your experience for you to heal completely. Your healing belongs to you.

Walking away is a victory. Every day that you choose your peace over their chaos, your truth over their lies, and your future over their manipulation is a victory. You don't need to defeat them; you just need to choose yourself, rinse, and repeat.

The Cat wants you to believe that the game can only end on their terms, with their permission, or through their acknowledgment. You are not their hostage; you are not stuck. Truth is, *you* hold the power to end the game at any moment simply by refusing to play.

Your Final Declarations

As you step into this new chapter of your life, it's powerful to make some final declarations—not to your abuser, but to yourself. These aren't statements you need to say out loud (unless you want to) or share with anyone else. They're internal commitments that solidify your transformation and anchor your new reality.

Declarations of Identity:

I am not a victim; I am a survivor who thrives. My identity is not defined by what was done to me but by how I've grown through it.

I am not broken; I am Beautifully restored to my original brilliance. The cracks in my life have been filled with golden confidence, self-worth, and God's love.

I am not damaged goods; I am a Woman with a story. My experiences have given me wisdom, empathy, and strength that make me more valuable in relationships, not less.

I am not too much; I was just with the wrong person. My intensity, my emotions, my needs, and my standards aren't flaws to be minimized but gifts to be honored.

I am not hard to love; I was just loving someone incapable of receiving it. My capacity for love is a strength, not a weakness, when directed toward someone worthy of it.

Declarations of Boundaries:

I will never again accept crumbs and call it a feast. That wasn't it. I know what real love looks like now, and I won't settle for counterfeits.

I will never again explain my worth to someone determined to discount it. My value is no longer up for debate or negotiation.

I will never again set myself on fire to keep someone else warm. Self-sacrifice that destroys me serves no one.

I will never again make someone a priority who's made me a last resort. I am more than someone's convenient option. Reciprocity is not a dirty word, but a part of my everyday vocabulary for future healthy relationships.

I will never again ignore red flags disguised as red carpet. When flattery, love, and rapid affection are rolled out before me, I won't miss the hidden flag poles. I trust my instincts now and honor what they tell me.

Declarations of Future:

I will build a life so Beautiful that I'm not looking for someone else to complete me. My life is full, whole, and meaningful on its own.

I will use my story to help other women recognize their worth and escape their own cat-and-mouse games. My experience becomes an escape route for others.

I will love myself first, completely, and most consistently; the love from others will be a bonus, not my sole source.

I will trust God's plan for my life, knowing that my past pain is being transformed into future purpose. My story isn't over; it's just beginning.

I will walk in the confidence of a woman who knows her worth, owns her power, and trusts her journey. I am no longer seeking validation; I am living from a place of inner knowing.

Connecting with Becoming

One of the most powerful aspects of declaring "game over" is connecting with the woman you're becoming. She's not some distant, perfect version of yourself—she's the natural evolution of who you are right now, informed by everything you've learned and strengthened by everything you've overcome.

And the best part is, you can tap into "her" wisdom and strength right now, even when you feel lost, doubtful, or weak. Like me, you may experience days when you want to run back to the familiarity of the game, but ask yourself, "What would a healed and whole me do?"

The Woman You're Becoming:

She knows her worth without needing external validation. She's not seeking approval or trying to prove her value to anyone. She simply knows who she is and what she brings to the world.

She trusts her instincts completely. She's learned to distinguish between fear and intuition, between past trauma and present wisdom. When something doesn't feel right, she honors that feeling.

She chooses peace over drama every time. She's not interested in chaos, conflict, or emotional roller coasters. She values stability, consistency, and calm.

She loves herself first and most consistently. She's not waiting for someone else to love her properly; she's already doing that for herself. Any love she receives from others is a bonus, not a necessity.

She uses her voice without apology. She speaks her truth, sets her boundaries, and expresses her needs clearly and confidently. She's not afraid of being "too much" for the wrong people.

She builds a life she loves. She's not waiting for someone to rescue her or complete her. She's creating a Beautiful, meaningful life that she's excited to wake up to every day.

She helps other women find their way. She uses her story, her wisdom, and her strength to help other women recognize their worth and escape their own toxic situations.

Other Questions to Ask Your Future Self:

- What would she do in this situation?
- How would she handle this challenge?
- What boundaries would she set?
- What choices would she make?
- How would she treat herself?
- What would she say to someone trying to diminish her worth?

Your future self isn't faultless, but she's free. She's not without challenges, but she faces them from a place of strength rather than fear. She's not without scars, but she wears them as evidence of her Tenacity and resilience rather than shame.

The Beautiful truth is that the woman you're becoming is already within you. Every time you choose yourself, set a boundary, trust your instincts, or refuse to accept less than you deserve, you're becoming her.

Cat Tactics Decoded

The Hoover Maneuver: Even after you've declared "game over," the Cat may hoover around you, attempting to pull you back in with promises of change, declarations of love, or manufactured crises. No one needs a loan or a place to stay faster than a Cat when the Mouse decides to exit the game. Remember that this is just another tactic, not evidence of genuine transformation.

The Smear Campaign Finale: When the Cat realizes they've truly lost control, they may launch a final smear campaign to damage your reputation or turn others against you. For me, this was a concerted phone campaign to family members and allies to disparage my character. Know that your character will speak for itself; don't waste energy defending any lies.

The Replacement Strategy: The Cat may quickly move on to a new narcissistic supply and flaunt this relationship to make you jealous or doubt your decision. Hopefully, this doesn't happen on social media for you like it did for me, but there's no low too low for the Cat. Remember that you're not being replaced; you're being freed, and you should pity their new target, not envy her.

Mouse Traps

The Closure Trap: You believe you need a final conversation, apology, or acknowledgment from your abuser to truly move on. Closure comes from within, not from them.

The Guilt Trap: You feel guilty for "giving up" on the relationship or worry that you didn't try hard enough. But you tried more than enough; some people are not capable of giving or receiving healthy love.

The Rescue Fantasy Trap: You hope that by leaving, you'll shock them into changing, and they'll come back as the person you always knew they could be. People change when they want to, not when you leave.

The Monitoring Trap: You continue to check their social media, ask mutual friends about them, or otherwise keep tabs on their life. This keeps you emotionally connected to someone you're trying to disconnect from.

Walking Away with Your Head Held High

The final act of declaring "game over" isn't about them at all. It's about you choosing to honor your worth, protect your peace, and invest your energy in building the life you deserve rather than trying to fix someone you didn't create or break.

You're walking away not because you're weak, but because you're strong enough to choose yourself. You're refusing to accept less than you deserve. Yes, you believe in love, but you believe in that real love, the kind that's allergic to counterfeits.

You're walking away as a High-value woman who knows her worth, a high-scoring woman who has learned the game and chosen not to play. You're walking away with your dignity intact, your lessons learned, and your future so bright.

The Cat-and-mouse game is over, and you won - not by defeating your opponent, but by finally returning the invitation to play back to the sender.

In the next chapter, we'll explore how to reclaim joy as an act of resistance against the abuse you've endured. We'll discover how celebration and happiness become essential components of your healing journey, not frivolous luxuries you don't deserve.

For now, remember: you were always Woman—Beautiful, Intelligent, Tenacious, Courageous, with High-value. You were always worthy of love, respect, and kindness. The game couldn't change that truth; it could only temporarily obscure it.

Now you can see clearly. Now you know your worth. Now you're free.

Game over. Roll the credits.

18

Chapter 18: Reclaiming Joy: The Happiness Resistance

"You make known to me the path of life; you will fill me with joy in your presence, with eternal pleasures at your right hand." - Psalm 16:11 NIV

There's something revolutionary about a woman who has survived emotional terrorism choosing to be happy. How dare you decide that joy is not only possible but necessary! How Courageous of you to refuse to let your past pain define your present and future possibilities!

Your abuser wanted to steal many things from you: your confidence, your identity, your sense of reality, your ability to trust. But perhaps the cruelest theft of all was the theft of your joy.

They convinced you that happiness was selfish, that laughter was inappropriate, that feeling good about yourself was arrogant. The Cat taught you that your natural state should be anxiety and worry, that peace was temporary, and that joy was something you had to earn through purr-fect behavior.

They were wrong about all of that, but they were especially wrong about this.

Joy is not a luxury you can't afford. Happiness is not frivolous or selfish. The pursuit of both is not only your right; it's your resistance. Every moment you choose joy over despair, happiness over misery, celebration over self-punishment, you are declaring jihad on all the lies that once held you captive.

This chapter is about reclaiming what was stolen from you. It's about understanding that your capacity for joy, happiness, and abundance is not only intact but is actually evidence of your strength, your resilience, and your refusal to be broken by what you've endured. It's about learning to see joy and happiness not as rewards you have to earn, but as birthrights you get to claim.

Understanding Joy vs. Happiness: Both Matter

Before we dive into reclaiming these essential parts of your soul, it's important to understand the difference between joy and happiness, and why both are crucial to your healing and thriving.

Happiness is an emotion, a feeling that comes and goes based on circumstances. It's the delight you feel when something good happens, the contentment you experience when life is going well, the pleasure you take in simple moments. Happiness is circumstantial, temporary, and often dependent on external factors.

Joy, however, is deeper than happiness. It's a state of being, a settled confidence in your worth and God's goodness that exists regardless of circumstances around you. Joy can coexist with sadness, pain, or difficulty. How is that? Because joy is the unshakable knowledge that you are loved, valued, and destined for good things, even when life is hard.

Both happiness and joy were targets of the Cat's campaign against your well-being:

They attacked your happiness by:

- Creating chaos that prevented you from enjoying simple pleasures
- Punishing you for being happy or excited about anything
- Convincing you that you didn't deserve good things
- Making you feel guilty for experiencing any positive emotions, especially when *they* were sad
- Ensuring that any happiness you felt was temporary, conditional, and

controlled

They attacked your joy by:

- Undermining your sense of worth and identity
- Convincing you that you were fundamentally flawed or unlovable
- Creating an environment where peace and safety were impossible
- Teaching you that your value was dependent on their approval
- Making you believe that suffering and sacrifice were the least you could do

Reclaiming both happiness and joy is essential because they serve different functions in your healing and thriving. Happiness helps you enjoy the present moment and find delight in everyday experiences. Joy gives you the strength to endure difficult times and the confidence to believe in your future.

Joy as Your Birthright

One of the first lies you need to reject is that joy is something you have to earn. Your abuser convinced you that joy was conditional on your performance, your behavior, and your ability to make and keep them happy. They taught you that joy was a reward for good behavior and that it could be taken away at any moment if you displeased them.

This is not how joy works. Joy is not a performance bonus. It's not a prize you win or a privilege you earn. Joy is your birthright as a beloved child of God.

Biblical Foundation for Joy:

- "The joy of the Lord is your strength" (Nehemiah 8:10)
- "I have told you this so that my joy may be in you and that your joy may be complete" (John 15:11)
- "Weeping may stay for the night, but joy comes in the morning" (Psalm 30:5)

God didn't create you to live in perpetual sadness, anxiety, or fear. He created you for joy, for delight, for the full experience of abundant living. Your capacity for joy is not a flaw to be corrected or a weakness to be exploited. It's a gift to be celebrated and a strength to be cultivated.

Reclaiming Your Right to Joy:

Joy in your identity. You are fearfully and wonderfully made (Psalm 139:14). Your existence brings God joy, which means you have inherent worth that no one can diminish or destroy.

Joy in your survival. You survived something that could have destroyed you. Your Tenacity, your strength, and your refusal to give up are all reasons for joy, not shame.

Joy in your growth. Every step you've taken toward healing, every boundary you've set, every moment you've chosen yourself over someone else's comfort is cause for celebration.

Joy in your future. Your past is not the blueprint for your future. You have unlimited potential for growth, love, connection, and contribution. Your story is still being written, and the best chapters are yet to come.

Taking a Happiness Inventory

One of the most powerful exercises in reclaiming joy and happiness is taking inventory of what actually brings you delight. Once it has settled in your soul that you *deserve* delight, it makes the pursuit of joy and happiness that much more important. If you're like me, during all that toxicity, you likely lost touch with your *own* preferences, desires, and sources of happiness. I remember being so focused on pleasing to avoid pain, I forgot how to pursue the pleasure joy brings.

Rediscover Your Happiness Sources:

Simple pleasures. What small things bring you joy? A cup of coffee with your favorite cream flavor in the morning? The smell of flowers? A good book? Soft blankets? Music that makes you want to dance? Can you imagine for me it was pancakes with crispy edges lol? Start noticing and honoring these simple (and quirky) sources of happiness.

Sensory delights. What feels good to your body? Warm baths? Massage? Soft textures? Beautiful colors? Delicious food? Your body was created to welcome pleasure, not pain.

Creative expression. What allows you to express your creativity? Writing? Painting? Singing? Dancing? Cooking? Sewing? Gardening? Creative expression is one of the most direct paths to joy because it connects you with your divine nature as a creator.

Connection and community. Who cracks you up without trying? Who accepts you exactly as you are? Who celebrates your victories and comforts you in your struggles? Healthy relationships are a primary source of both happiness and joy.

Achievement and growth. What gives you a sense of accomplishment? Learning something new? Completing a project? Helping someone else? Overcoming a challenge? Recognizing your own growth and celebrating your achievements is essential for sustained happiness.

Spiritual practices. What connects you with God and fills you with peace? Prayer? Worship? Reading Scripture? Being in nature? Serving others? Spiritual practices and disciplines often provide the deepest and most lasting joy.

Create Your Happiness Plan:

Once you've identified what brings you happiness, create a plan to incorporate these things into your daily and weekly routine. This isn't selfish or frivolous. It's essential maintenance for your mental, emotional, and spiritual well-being after emotional abuse.

Daily happiness habits. Choose 2-3 small things you can do every day that bring you joy. Maybe it's listening to music while you get ready, taking a few minutes to appreciate nature, or calling someone who makes you laugh.

Weekly happiness practices. Plan one or two activities each week that you genuinely enjoy. This might be a hobby, time with friends, a special meal, or an activity that brings you peace.

Monthly happiness adventures. Once a month, do something that brings you significant joy. This could be a day trip, going to a special event, trying something new, or indulging in something you love.

Seasonal happiness celebrations. Plan special ways to celebrate holidays, seasons, and personal milestones. Create new traditions that reflect your values and bring you joy.

Overcoming Guilt About Happiness

One of the biggest obstacles to reclaiming joy and happiness is the guilt you feel when you experience positive emotions. The Cat may have conditioned you to feel guilty about being happy, and that conditioning may not disappear overnight.

Common Guilt Messages:

- "I don't deserve to be happy after what I've been through."
- "It's selfish to focus on my own happiness when others are suffering."
- "I should be working on healing, not having fun."
- "If I'm happy, people will think I'm over what happened to me."
- "I feel guilty being happy when my abuser is probably miserable."
- "Happy people are shallow and don't understand real pain."

Re-framing Guilt About Happiness:

Your happiness doesn't diminish other people's pain. You being miserable doesn't help anyone else who is suffering. Likewise, your suffering can't help anyone who won't get help. But your joy and healing can be a beacon of hope for others who are still struggling and want to be free.

Happiness is part of healing, not separate from it. Joy and happiness aren't distractions from your healing work; they're essential components of it. You can't heal into wholeness while rejecting fundamental parts of your worthiness—you are worthy of joy and happiness.

You deserve happiness because you're human, not because you've earned

it. Your worthiness for joy and happiness isn't based on your performance, your past, or your pain. It's based on your inherent value as a person created in God's image.

Your happiness is an act of resistance. Every moment you choose joy over despair, you're refusing to let the Cat's abuse continue to ripple through your life. Your happiness is proof that they didn't succeed in destroying you.

Happiness gives you the strength to help others. When you're operating from a place of joy and fulfillment, you have more to offer others. You can't pour from an empty cup, and happiness helps keep your cup full.

Celebration as Healing

Celebration is one of the most powerful and underutilized tools in the healing process. Your abuser likely punished you for celebrating yourself, your achievements, or your joy. They may have minimized your successes, ignored your accomplishments, or made you feel guilty for being proud of yourself.

Reclaiming your right to celebrate yourself is a chain-breaking activity that frees you to pursue every joyful moment you can stand.

Why Celebration Heals:

It rewires your brain for positivity. When you celebrate good things, you're training your brain to notice and appreciate positive experiences instead of only focusing on problems and pain.

It builds self-worth. Celebrating your achievements, growth, and positive qualities helps you internalize your own value instead of depending on others for validation.

It creates positive memories. Celebration creates joyful memories that can sustain you during difficult times and remind you that life is filled with beauty and goodness.

It connects you with others. Sharing celebrations with people who care about you strengthens relationships and builds community around joy instead of just trauma.

It honors your journey. Celebrating milestones in your healing acknowledges how far you've come and motivates you to continue growing.

What to Celebrate—EVERYTHING!

Healing milestones. Every step forward in your healing journey deserves recognition. Celebrate the first day you don't think about the Cat, the first time you set a boundary, the first time you choose yourself over someone else's comfort.

Personal achievements. Celebrate your accomplishments, both big and small. Being time-challenged, if I made it to all appointments *early* in a day, that deserved confetti. Getting a promotion, finishing a book, learning a new skill, or simply getting through a difficult day are all worthy of celebration.

Relationship victories. Celebrate healthy relationships, meaningful connections, and moments of genuine intimacy and trust. These are precious gifts that deserve recognition.

Creative expressions. Celebrate your creativity, whether it's writing a poem, cooking a delicious meal, decorating your space, or any other way you express your unique gifts.

Acts of courage. Celebrate every time you choose Courage over comfort, truth over convenience, or growth over stagnation. These choices require tremendous bravery and deserve recognition.

Simple joys. Celebrate the small moments that bring you happiness: a Beautiful sunset, a good laugh with a friend, a peaceful morning, a moment of gratitude.

Cat Tactics Decoded

The Joy Punishment: The Cat systematically punished you for experiencing joy, happiness, or excitement about anything that didn't center around them. They taught you that positive emotions were dangerous and that expressing happiness would result in criticism, withdrawal, or sabotage.

The Happiness Hijacking: The Cat inserted themselves into every source of happiness in your life, either by taking full or partial credit for it, controlling it, or destroying it. They wanted to be your only source of positive emotions so they could control your emotional state completely.

The Celebration Sabotage: The Cat consistently ruined special occasions, achievements, and moments of joy by creating drama, picking fights, or giving you the silent treatment. They taught you that celebration was dangerous and no match for their kill switch.

Mouse Traps

The Guilt Trap: You feel guilty for being happy when others are still suffering or you "should" be focused on healing. Remember that your happiness doesn't diminish anyone else's pain, and joy is actually essential for complete healing.

The Perfection Trap: You believe you need to be completely healed before you deserve to be happy. Healing and happiness can coexist, and in fact, happiness often accelerates the healing process.

The Shallow Trap: You worry that focusing on happiness makes you shallow or means you're not taking your trauma seriously. True depth includes the full range of human emotions, including joy and happiness.

The Temporary Trap: You're afraid to invest in happiness because you believe it will be taken away from you again. While individual moments of happiness are temporary, your capacity for joy is permanent and can't be destroyed by external circumstances.

Building a Life of Sustainable Joy

Reclaiming joy and happiness isn't about forcing yourself to be positive all the time or pretending that life is always wonderful. It's about creating a life that naturally generates more joy than sorrow, more hope than despair, more love than fear.

Your pursuit of joy and happiness is not selfish, frivolous, or inappropriate. It's revolutionary. It's your declaration that you refuse to be defined by what was done to you. It's your commitment to living fully, loving deeply, and experiencing all the beauty that life has to offer.

Every moment you choose joy, you're writing a new chapter in your story.

Every time you allow yourself to be happy, you're validating that your abuser's attempts to destroy your spirit failed. Every celebration, every laugh, every moment of pure delight is evidence that you are not just surviving but thriving.

In the next chapter, we'll explore how to rewrite your love story and create new narratives about relationships, romance, and your capacity to give and receive healthy love. We'll discover how your experience with emotional terrorism, while painful, has actually equipped you with wisdom and discernment that can lead to deeper, more authentic connections than you ever thought possible.

For now, remember: your joy is your resistance, your happiness breaks chains, and your celebration is your victory song.

19

Chapter 19: Rewriting Your Love Story

"Above all else, guard your heart, for everything you do flows from it." - Proverbs 4:23 NIV

Sis, you deserve real love. Not the counterfeit version you tolerated. Not the crumbs disguised as a feast. Not the emotional terrorism wrapped in occasional angry days off.

You deserve the kind of love that sees you, knows you, celebrates you, and chooses you again and again.

But before you can receive that love, you have to believe you're worthy of it. Before you can recognize healthy love, you have to understand what it actually looks like. Before you can create a brand new love story, it's necessary to heal from the old one and learn to love yourself first.

This chapter isn't about finding your next relationship. It's about becoming the kind of woman who attracts healthy love when it's time because she already knows her worth. It's about rewriting your entire understanding of what love looks like, feels like, and acts like. It's about creating standards so high and boundaries so strong that only genuine love can reach you.

Your past relationship wasn't loving, even though it felt like it at times. It was addiction, trauma bonding, and emotional manipulation disguised as romance. Real love doesn't require you to lose yourself, walk on eggshells, or earn affection through perfect behavior. Real love doesn't punish you for having needs, questions, opinions, or boundaries.

The love story you're going to write from now on will be different because you are different. You've been through the fire and emerged stronger, wiser, and more discerning. You know what you won't tolerate because you've lived through the consequences of tolerating the intolerable. You know your worth because you've experienced the cost of giving it away for free.

The Foundation: Learning to Love Yourself First

Before you can create a healthy romantic relationship, you must first create a healthy relationship with yourself. This isn't selfish; it's essential. You cannot give what you don't have. If you don't love yourself, you'll accept poor treatment from others because it matches your internal relationship with yourself.

What Self-Love Actually Means:

Self-love isn't narcissism, selfishness, or thinking you're better than everyone else. It's treating yourself with the same kindness, respect, and care that you would show to someone you deeply love. It's recognizing your inherent worth and refusing to accept treatment that contradicts that worth.

Self-love is setting boundaries. You protect your time, energy, and emotional well-being because you recognize they're valuable and finite resources.

Self-love is honoring your needs. You acknowledge that your needs matter and you take responsibility for meeting them instead of expecting others to read your mind or rescue you.

Self-love is speaking to yourself with kindness. You become aware of your internal dialogue and choose to speak to yourself with compassion rather than criticism.

Self-love is investing in your growth. You prioritize your healing, learning, and development because you believe you're worth the investment.

Self-love is celebrating your victories. You acknowledge your progress, your strengths, and your accomplishments instead of minimizing them or focusing only on what you still need to improve.

Self-love is forgiving your mistakes. You extend grace to yourself when you fall short, recognizing that mistakes are part of being human, not evidence of your unworthiness.

Build Your Self-Love Foundation:

Daily self-care practices. Create routines that nourish your body, mind, and spirit. This might include exercise, healthy eating, adequate sleep, meditation, prayer, or activities that bring you joy.

Positive self-talk. Notice when you're being self-critical and consciously choose to speak to yourself with kindness. Ask yourself: "Would I talk to my best friend this way?"

Boundary practice. Start setting small boundaries in low-stakes situations to build your boundary-setting muscle. Practice saying no without justifying, over-explaining, or apologizing.

Personal goal setting. Set goals that are about your own growth and fulfillment, not about pleasing others or proving your worth.

Solitude appreciation. Learn to enjoy your own company. Take yourself on dates, pursue hobbies you enjoy, and become comfortable being alone without feeling lonely.

Values clarification. Identify what's truly important to you and make decisions based on your values rather than others' expectations or approval.

Understanding What Real Love Looks Like

After experiencing emotional terrorism, your understanding of love may be distorted. You might mistake intensity for intimacy, jealousy for passion, or control for care. Learning to recognize healthy love is crucial for rewriting your love story. Consider this.

Characteristics of Real Love:

Real love is consistent. It doesn't fluctuate based on mood, circumstances, or your behavior. You don't have to earn it daily or worry about losing it if you make a mistake.

Real love is respectful. It honors your boundaries, values your opinions even when they differ, and treats you as an equal partner rather than a subordinate.

Real love is supportive. It encourages your growth, celebrates your successes, and provides comfort during difficult times without trying to fix or change you.

Real love is secure. It doesn't create anxiety, fear, or the need to constantly prove your worth. You feel safe to be yourself without fear of punishment or withdrawal.

Real love is honest. It communicates directly and kindly, addresses problems constructively, and doesn't use manipulation, lies, or games to get needs met.

Real love is patient. It doesn't rush you, pressure you, or demand immediate change, satisfaction, or commitment. It allows the relationship to develop naturally at a pace that feels comfortable for both people.

Real love is empowering. It makes you feel more like yourself, not less. It encourages your independence, supports your goals, and celebrates your individuality.

Real love is reciprocal. Both partners give and receive, support and are supported, love and are loved. The relationship feels balanced rather than one-sided.

What Real Love Is NOT:

Real love is not conditional. It doesn't withdraw affection as punishment or use love as a reward for good behavior.

Real love is not dramatic. It doesn't create constant chaos, crisis, or emotional turmoil. Healthy relationships are generally peaceful and stable.

Real love is not jealous. It doesn't try to isolate you from friends and family. It celebrates you without comparison or competition.

Real love is not demanding. It doesn't require you to sacrifice your identity, personality, or values to maintain the relationship.

Real love is not rushed. It doesn't pressure you for commitment, intimacy, or major life decisions before you're ready.

Red Flags: Your Early Warning System

Now, when you see a red carpet laid out for you, you're checking for missing flag poles. Your experience with emotional terrorism has given you valuable knowledge about what to avoid in future relationships. Trust your instincts and pay attention to red flags, even if they seem small or if the person has other appealing qualities.

Major Red Flags to Never Ignore:

Love-bombing. Fast, excessive attention, affection, and declarations of love very early in the relationship. This feels amazing, but remember it's often a manipulation tactic designed to create quick attachment.

Boundary violations. Pushing against your boundaries, ignoring your "no," or making you feel guilty for having limits. This shows a lack of respect for your autonomy.

Isolation attempts. Trying to separate you from friends, family, or activities you enjoy. This is often disguised as wanting to spend more time together or concern for your well-being.

Controlling behavior. Wanting to know where you are at all times, checking your phone, making decisions for you, or trying to control your appearance, behavior, or choices.

Emotional manipulation. Using guilt trips, silent treatment, threats, or emotional outbursts to get their way. This includes playing victim to avoid accountability when confronted about their behavior.

Inconsistent behavior. Being wonderful one day and cold or cruel the next, creating confusion and keeping you off-balance.

Disrespect for your values. Mocking, dismissing, or trying to change your beliefs, values, or things that are important to you.

Financial control. Trying to control your money, prevent you from working, or create financial dependence early in the relationship.

Sexual pressure. Unwelcome or inappropriate touch, pushing for physical intimacy, ignoring or making you feel guilty for your sexual boundaries.

Substance abuse. Excessive drinking, drug use, or other addictive behaviors that affect their judgment and behavior.

Trust Your Gut:

If something feels off, it probably is. Don't ignore your instincts because you want the relationship to work, or because you can't put your finger on *exactly* what's wrong. Time spent with God and getting to know yourself will strengthen your discernment muscle for moments of clarity. What are some common gut feelings that signal problems?

- Feeling like you're walking on eggshells
- Constantly second-guessing yourself
- Feeling anxious or drained after spending time together
- Feeling like you need to hide parts of yourself
- Feeling like you're always trying to prove your worth
- Feeling confused about where you stand in the relationship

Green Lights: What to Look For

Just as important as recognizing red flags is learning to recognize green lights—the positive qualities and behaviors that indicate someone might be capable of healthy love. Based on your experience and your growing self-love, it's time to create clear standards for what you will and won't accept in romantic relationships. These aren't unrealistic expectations; they're basic requirements for healthy love. What are your new non-negotiables?

Green Lights in Healthy Relationships:

Emotional maturity. They can regulate their own emotions, communicate their needs directly, and handle conflict constructively without resorting to manipulation or emotional outbursts.

Respect for boundaries. They accept your "no" gracefully, respect your limits, and don't try to push or manipulate you into changing your mind.

Consistent behavior. Their words match their actions, and their behavior is relatively consistent over time. You don't feel like you're dealing with different people from day to day.

Support for your independence. They encourage your friendships, support your goals, and celebrate your successes without feeling threatened or trying to compete.

Healthy conflict resolution. They can disagree with you respectfully, work through problems constructively, and apologize sincerely when they make mistakes.

Personal responsibility. They take ownership of their mistakes, work on their own issues, and don't blame others for their problems or emotions.

Shared values. While you don't need to agree on everything, you share core values about important things like honesty, respect, family, faith, and how to treat others.

Emotional availability. They're present in conversations, interested in your thoughts and feelings, and capable of emotional intimacy without becoming overwhelmed or withdrawn.

Growth mindset. They're committed to personal growth, open to feedback, and willing to work on themselves and the relationship.

Mutual effort. Both people should be investing in the relationship and working to meet each other's needs.

Balanced give and take. Sometimes you'll give more, sometimes they will, but over time, it should feel relatively balanced.

Shared decision-making. Major decisions that affect both of you are made together, with both people's input valued.

Physical and emotional intimacy. Both people should respect and feel comfortable with each other's boundaries for intimacy.

Future compatibility. You share similar goals and visions for the future, or at least are able to compromise and support each other's dreams.

Fun and enjoyment. The relationship brings joy, laughter, and pleasure to your life, not just stress and drama.

The Dating Process: Taking Your Time

After emotional terrorism, it's crucial to take dating slowly and intentionally. You're not looking for just anyone; you're looking for someone who deserves access to your heart and life.

Healthy Dating Principles to Start:

Begin with friendship. Get to know someone as a person before considering them as a romantic partner. Friendship provides a solid foundation for lasting love.

Take it slow. Don't rush into physical or emotional intimacy. Take time to observe their character, consistency, and compatibility over time.

Maintain your independence. Continue investing in your own life, friendships, and goals. Don't lose yourself in the excitement of a new relationship.

Observe their character. Actions over words. Pay attention to how they treat service workers, talk about their exes, handle stress, and respond to disappointment. Character is revealed in small moments.

Meet their people. Healthy people have healthy relationships. Meet their friends and family to get a broader picture of who they are, who they attract, and how they function in relationships.

Discuss important topics. Have conversations about values, goals, deal-breakers, and expectations before you're too emotionally invested to think clearly.

Trust your instincts. If something feels off, don't ignore it. If you feel pressured, confused, or anxious, pay attention to those feelings.

Maintain your standards. Remember your foundations for self-love and real love earlier in this chapter. Don't lower or compromise your standards because you're lonely, because they have *other* good qualities, or because you're afraid you won't find anyone else.

'New' Cat Tactics Decoded

The Rebound Rush: A new Cat might try to rush you into a relationship before you've fully healed from your previous abuse. They present themselves as your rescuer and try to create quick attachments before you have time to see their true character.

The False Green Light: A manipulative person might initially display green light behaviors to gain your trust, then gradually reveal their true nature once you're emotionally invested. When a green light turns yellow, it's a warning that it will eventually turn red. This is why taking time and observing consistency is so important.

The Healing Hijack: A new Cat might try to position themselves as essential to your healing process, making you feel like you *need* them to complete your recovery. Healthy partners support your healing but don't try to become the center of it.

Mouse Traps

The Loneliness Trap: You settle for less than you deserve because you're afraid of being alone. Remember that being alone is better than being with someone who doesn't value you.

The Gratitude Trap: You're so grateful that someone is interested in you that you ignore red flags or lower your standards. Your worth isn't determined by someone else's interest in you.

The Comparison Trap: You compare your new relationship to your abusive one and think that anything better is good enough. Or, the comparison begins to punish the new Cat for the behavior of the old. Don't let your past trauma lower your standards or ruin the opportunity for healthy love.

The Rescue Trap: You try to save or fix someone who shows potential but isn't actually ready for a healthy relationship. You can't love someone into health, and trying will exhaust you and uproot all of the hard work you've poured into your healing journey.

Your New Love Story Begins Now

Your new love story doesn't begin when you meet the right person. It begins now, with you! Learning to love yourself, establishing healthy standards, refusing to accept anything less than genuine love—this is the once upon a time you've been waiting for.

This story might include periods of singleness while you continue healing and growing. It might include dating experiences that lead to ghosts or teach you valuable lessons about what you want and don't want. There may be chapters that include false starts and disappointments as you learn to navigate healthy relationships.

But ultimately, your new love story is about you becoming the kind of woman who attracts and maintains healthy love because she knows her worth, honors her needs, and refuses to settle for counterfeits. Here are a few love story affirmations to pack for the pages ahead:

- I deserve real love, not just any love
- I am worthy of respect, kindness, and consistency
- I will not settle for less than I deserve out of fear or loneliness
- I trust my instincts and honor my boundaries
- I am complete on my own and choose to share my life, not give it away
- I attract healthy love because I love myself first
- My past does not determine my future in love

The woman you are now—stronger, wiser, more discerning—is capable of creating a love story more Beautiful than anything you have ever imagined. You know what you won't tolerate because you've lived through the consequences of dishonoring that small voice. You know your own worth because you've stopped allowing others to stick *their* price tag on you.

In the final chapter, we'll explore how to transform from surviving to fully thriving. You'll learn how to embrace your post-traumatic growth, reclaim your dreams, and build an unstoppable future legacy.

For now, remember: you are not looking for someone to save you. You are looking for someone worthy of the woman you've become.

20

Chapter 20: Surviving to Thriving: Repossess Abundant Life

"The thief comes only to steal and kill and destroy; I have come that they may have life, and have it abundantly." - John 10:10 NIV

There comes a moment in every survivor's journey when you realize that healing isn't really the end goal—it's the beginning. You made the tough decision to break free, process the trauma, and rebuild your sense of self. You've learned to set boundaries, reclaim your joy, and love yourself first. You've survived the worst that emotional terrorism and narcissistic abuse could throw at you.

But survival was never meant to be your final destination. You were created for more than just getting by, more than just healing and "moving on" from what was done to you, more than just avoiding an encore of abuse. You were created for abundance, for purpose, for a life so full and meaningful that your past pain becomes the foundation for your future impact.

This is where surviving transforms into thriving. At this stage in your growth, you're too Intelligent to settle for survival alone. You did more than conquer narcissistic abuse. This is where your story shifts from what happened *to* you to what you're going to *do* with what you've learned. This is where you repossess the abundant life that was always meant to be yours.

Your band of thieves—the Cat in cahoots with Leviathan, the childhood trauma, the negative self-talk, your own limiting beliefs—came to steal your dreams, kill your hope, and destroy your sense of purpose. But you're still here. You're still dreaming. You're still hoping. You're still believing that your life can be more than just a recovery story.

Paramount to Jesus' purpose was abundant life, a life that overflows with love, joy, and meaning. Not a life free from challenges, but a life so rich in His glory that the challenges become opportunities for growth, service, and deeper connection with both God and others. This abundant life isn't just available to those who have life figured out; it's available to you, right now, exactly as you are, with all your Beautiful scabs and scars.

Understanding Post-Traumatic Growth

To begin a deeper dive into the transition from surviving to thriving, let's take a look at the concept of *post-traumatic growth*. First developed by psychologists Richard Tedeschi and Lawrence Calhoun (2004), post-traumatic growth challenges the assumption that *trauma only damages us*. Does your story end with what emotional terrorism stole, killed, or destroyed? No, Ma'am. What narcissistic abuse meant for evil, can you envision God working it out for your good? Of course! While trauma certainly causes pain, rewires our brains, and requires committed work to heal, it can also become a catalyst for profound positive change, increased resilience, and a deeper gratitude for living.

The Five Areas of Post-Traumatic Growth:

Appreciation of life. Survivors often develop a heightened appreciation for simple pleasures, everyday moments, and the gift of being alive. What once seemed ordinary becomes precious.

Relating to others. Many survivors develop deeper, more authentic relationships. Having experienced pain, they become more empathetic, more selective about who they allow into their lives, and more capable of genuine intimacy.

Awareness of personal strength. Surviving narcissistic abuse reveals inner strength you didn't know you had. You discover that you're capable of enduring more, growing more, and overcoming more than you ever imagined.

Spiritual development. Many survivors experience a deepened faith, understanding, and stronger relationship with God. Crisis often clarifies where your true Source of strength and help lies.

New possibilities. Trauma can shatter old assumptions about life and open up new possibilities for who you can become and what you can accomplish. Sometimes we have to lose our old life to discover our true life.

This isn't about being grateful for the traumatic behavior itself, but about recognizing that you've transformed something destructive into something constructive. You've converted pain into wisdom, suffering into strength, and trauma into triumph.

Discovering Your Purpose

One of the most powerful aspects of moving from surviving to thriving is discovering your unique purpose—the reason you're here, the contribution only you can make, the way your specific combination of experiences, gifts, and passions can serve the world.

Your purpose isn't separate from your pain; it often emerges from it. The very experiences that nearly destroyed you may become the foundation for your greatest contribution to others.

And don't be deceived, your purpose doesn't have to be grand and over-the-top. Your purpose doesn't have to involve starting a nonprofit, writing a bestselling book, or speaking on stage to thousands of people. It might be as simple as being the kind of mother who raises emotionally healthy children, the kind of friend who creates safe spaces for others to heal, or the kind of professional who treats everyone with dignity and respect.

Purpose is about alignment - living in a way that honors your values, uses your gifts, and contributes to something beyond yourself. It's about making your life count, not necessarily making it famous.

So, how do you find the path to discover your purpose? Try spending some quiet time in prayer and reflection with the questions below.

Purpose Discovery Questions:

What breaks your heart? Often our purpose is connected to the problems we feel most passionate about solving, the injustices that stir our souls, or the pain we feel called to heal.

What brings you alive? When do you feel most energized, most like yourself, most connected to something bigger than yourself? These moments often point toward your purpose.

What are your unique gifts? What comes naturally to you? What do others consistently ask for your help with? What abilities do you have that could serve others?

What have you learned that others need to know? Your experience with emotional terrorism has given you insights that could help other women avoid or escape similar situations. How might you share this wisdom?

What legacy do you want to leave? How do you want to be remembered? What impact do you want to have on the world? What would you regret *not* doing if you knew you only had a year to live?

Reclaiming Your Dreams

Emotional terrorism didn't just attack your past and present; it attacked your future. The Cat likely discouraged your dreams, minimized your goals, or convinced you that you weren't capable of achieving what you wanted. Part of thriving involves reclaiming those dreams and discovering new ones.

So, let this be your clarion call to rescue every dream held hostage by the emotional terrorist. You want it all back, and here's a great place to start. It's time to break your dreams free.

Dreams the Abuse Stole:

Career aspirations. Did they discourage you from pursuing education, career advancement, or professional goals? Did they make you feel like you weren't smart enough, capable enough, or deserving enough to achieve your ambitions?

Creative expressions. Did they mock your artistic interests, discourage your creativity, or make you feel like your creative pursuits were worthless or selfish?

Personal goals. Did they sabotage your health goals, financial goals, or personal development efforts? Did they make you feel guilty for investing in yourself?

Relationship dreams. Did they convince you that you weren't worthy of healthy love, authentic friendships, or supportive family relationships?

Adventure and experiences. Did they limit your travel, prevent you from trying new things, or make you feel like you didn't deserve to enjoy life while they were miserable?

The Reclaiming Process:

Acknowledge what was taken. Make a list of the dreams, goals, and aspirations that were discouraged, mocked, or sabotaged during the abusive relationship.

Grieve the lost time. Allow yourself to feel sad about the time that was lost, the opportunities that were missed, and the dreams that were deferred. Honest grief is valid and helpful.

Assess current relevance. Some dreams may no longer fit who you've become, and that's okay. Others may be more relevant than ever. Decide which dreams still call to you and which you're ready to release.

Start small. You don't have to achieve everything at once. Choose one dream to focus on and take one small step toward it. Progress creates momentum.

Expect resistance. Your own mind may resist pursuing dreams because it feels safer to stay small. This is normal. Push through the resistance with gentle persistence.

Celebrate progress. Acknowledge every step forward, no matter how small. You're not just pursuing a dream; you're reclaiming your *right* to dream.

Building Your Legacy

Thriving isn't just about creating a good life for yourself; it's about creating something that outlasts you. Your legacy is the impact you have on others, the positive change you create in the world, and the way you use your experience to make life better for those who come after you. Take a look at the types of legacy and follow these general principles to build a legacy for yourself that lasts.

Types of Legacy:

Personal legacy. The impact you have on your family, friends, and immediate community. This might involve raising healthy children, being a supportive friend, or creating a loving home environment.

Professional legacy. The contribution you make through your work, whether that's providing excellent service, mentoring others, or using your career to create positive change.

Service legacy. The ways you volunteer, give back, or serve causes that matter to you. This might involve helping other abuse survivors, supporting community organizations, or advocating for important issues.

Creative legacy. The art, writing, music, or other creative works you produce that inspire, encourage, or help others. Your story itself can be part of your creative legacy.

Wisdom legacy. The knowledge, insights, and wisdom you share with others, whether through formal teaching, informal mentoring, or simply living as an example of what's possible.

Legacy Building Principles:

Start where you are. You don't have to wait until you're "fully healed" or "completely successful" to start building your legacy. You can begin making a positive impact right now, exactly as you are.

Use your story. Your experience with emotional terrorism, while painful, has given you unique insights and empathy that can help others. Consider how your story might serve others who are still struggling.

Think generationally. How can you help ensure that the next generation of women is better equipped to recognize and avoid emotional terrorism? What else can you teach your daughters, nieces, or young women in your community?

Focus on multiplication. The greatest legacies are those that multiply - when you help one person who then helps another, it creates ripple effects that extend far beyond your direct influence.

Live your values. Your legacy isn't just what you accomplish; it's how you live. Embodying values like integrity, compassion, Courage, and authenticity creates a legacy that influences everyone you encounter.

The Abundant Life Jesus Offers

As a disciple of Christ, my heart won't let you leave this book without knowing *my* ultimate source for thriving after emotional terrorism. I wish that I intrinsically knew all of the strategies and best practices you just read about. I wish I had the I.T.C.—Intelligence, Tenacity, and the necessary Courage— to spring into action and fearlessly build my new life of purpose, reclaimed dreams, and legacy after enduring decades of narcissistic abuse. But that's not my story.

On January 8, 2022 when I heard those life-shattering words, "It's over. I want a divorce. We can divide up the bank accounts later", there was no abundant life to pursue because I was a dead woman walking. There was no broken heart to mend because my heart had driven off to move in with the other woman after what would be my last domestic violence encounter.

The moments, minutes, and days that followed weren't about thriving or abundance; it was all about staying here. If I could allow my mind and body to sleep while my spirit worshiped and prayed, I could stay alive. If I could muster up the strength and Courage to walk a thousand miles to grab my next breath, and do it again and again, I could stay alive in this *new* game.

You see, I was a pro at the game of cat-and-mouse, but the game of "life without the Cat"? Life without the chase, the drama, the toxicity, without the intermittent reinforcement of affection? "Where they do that at, God?!"

I'd been cast to play yet another role I didn't audition for—but I was chosen for.

And this time, I didn't have to learn my part by trial and error. Jesus held my hand. Jesus promised He wouldn't leave me nor forsake me, and kept that promise. If I would just shift all of the focus and attention and people-pleasing from the Cat to Him, i.e., kill the *idolatry* in my heart for the Cat and the game, He'd be the best provider, sustainer, restorer, protector-Husband I *never* had.

What did I have to lose? All of the pain, trauma, shame, disappointment, anger, frustration, and low self-esteem; nothing but love, peace, joy, Beauty, purpose, identity, and pure abundance to gain.

I surrendered the ashes of the life I once knew for the new, abundant life Jesus offered. An amazing opportunity for a divine glow up, not because I was so good, perfect, or deserving—but just because Jesus loved me that much. And, He loves you, too.

What does His abundant life look like? It wasn't about material wealth or worldly success—though He threw in those bonuses. It's about living with such deep security in God's love and my God-given identity that I was free to heal wholly, love myself first and others generously, serve joyfully, and pursue His purpose for me Courageously.

Elements of Abundant Life Through Christ:

Deep peace. Not the absence of conflict, but the presence of inner calm that comes from knowing you're loved, valued, and held by God regardless of circumstances.

Purposeful living. Understanding that your life has meaning and that you have a unique contribution to make to the world. Your experiences, including your painful ones, can be used for good.

Authentic relationships. The freedom to be genuinely yourself in relation-ships, to love and be loved without pretense or performance, and to experience the deep connection you were created for.

Generous heart. When you're secure in God's love and provision, you're free to give generously—not just money, but time, attention, encouragement, and support to others.

Unshakable hope. The confidence that your story isn't over, that God can work all things together for good, and that your future is bright regardless of your past.

Joy in the journey. The ability to find delight, Beauty, and meaning in everyday moments, not just in major achievements or milestones.

All these things and so much more are what it means for you to embrace the abundant life that Jesus offers. You can muster up your own grit and Tenacity to transition from surviving to thriving. For me, it was so much easier to rest and rely on the Creator of heaven and earth to create the abundant life I didn't have words to even ask for.

Living Abundantly Every Day

Abundant living isn't a destination you reach; it's your new theme song. It's the way you choose to move every day. It's about approaching each day with gratitude, purpose, and openness to the possibilities around you.

You are now free to create the life you want to live with new routines and practices. Your mornings may start with setting the day's intention of how you want to show up in the world, or how you want to impact others. You're able to regularly acknowledge the good things in your life, both big and small. You invest in relationships that are mutual, supportive, and life-giving. You use gratitude to shift your focus from what's lacking to what's abundant.

You realize the importance of rest and renewal. Abundant living includes abundant rest. What a difference taking care of your body, mind, and spirit through adequate sleep, relaxation, and restoration can make.

You've come so far from where you started. You've survived what felt un-survivable, learned what seemed unknowable, and grown in ways you never imagined possible. These are the fruits of your healing labor, bearing seeds that will keep feeding your growth, learning, and development.

You've transformed from victim to survivor to thriver.

For now, and always, remember: you weren't just saved from something; you were saved for something. Your abundant life is waiting for you to claim it and live it boldly.

Congratulations! Once upon a time starts—now.

Bibliography

Ronningstam, E. (2005). Identifying and Understanding the Narcissistic Personality. Oxford University Press.

Torgersen, S., Myers, J., Reichborn-Kjennerud, T., Røysamb, E., Kubarych, T. S., & Kendler, K. S. (2012). The heritability of Cluster B personality disorders assessed both by personal interview and questionnaire. Journal of Personality Disorders, 26(6), 848-866.

Pincus, A. L., Cain, N. M., & Wright, A. G. C. (2014). Narcissistic grandiosity and narcissistic vulnerability in psychotherapy. Personality Disorders: Theory, Research, and Treatment, 5(4), 439-443.

Winnicott, D. W. (1960). Ego distortion in terms of true and false self. In The Maturational Processes and the Facilitating Environment: Studies in the Theory of Emotional Development (pp. 140-152). International Universities Press.

Kernberg, O. F. (2018). Treatment of severe narcissistic pathology. American Psychiatric Association Publishing.

Tedeschi, R. G., & Calhoun, L. G. (2004). Post-traumatic growth: Conceptual foundations and empirical evidence. *Psychological Inquiry, 15*(1), 1-18.

A Prayer of Surrendered Ashes

Dear God,

This toxic, narcissistic relationship has burned everything to the ground with me inside.

My identity. My self-esteem. My hopes and dreams. It's all covered in ashes now, and I'm unable to put the pieces of me back together on my own. I need my Maker. Please show me how to surrender the ashes that surround me. Remind me of who You created me to be.

I picked up this book and read the testimony of a woman who You rescued from the devastation of narcissistic abuse, infidelity, manipulation, and abandonment.

Will You please do the same for me?

I, too, want to experience rebirth, renewal, and restoration.

Will You make me over, again?

My soul desperately needs a brand new foundation of love, joy, peace, and abundance. Help me to unlearn the toxic ways I've treated myself, and to teach others what the healed version of me expects. Give me the Courage to forgive myself, and release the "cat" from all resentment and offense. Restore the vibrant glow of an identity rooted in how You have always seen me—beautiful and wonderful.

You are a wiser, safer place for all the love I tried to pour on an idol. Pleasing You is a better use of my time and energy. So, to (begin, renew, or strengthen) our relationship, I ask forgiveness for my sins and shortcomings, and I believe that your son, Jesus, died for my sins and rose again. I confess with my mouth and believe with my heart that Jesus is Savior and Lord.

As Your beloved, nothing good will ever be withheld from me, and I can boldly come to You, without fear or judgment, any time I need Your help.

My journey to healing and freedom is protected by Your powerful hands, and every fearless step I take is secured under Your watchful eyes.

Thank you for the confidence to know that I am never alone, never forsaken. Your faithful actions will always match Your trusted word.

All praise and glory to the one and only Most High, who has sealed my freedom and opened my eyes to a life filled with goodness, mercy, and victory every day.

My heart is forever grateful.

Thank you, God.

Amen and selah.